An Independent
QUEBEC

The past, the present and the future

JACQUES PARIZEAU

An Independent
QUEBEC

The past, the present and the future

Translated by Robin Philpot

Baraka
Books

Original title: *La souveraineté du Québec, Hier, aujourd'hui et demain*
© 2009 Jacques Parizeau, Les editions Michel Brûlé
Publié avec l'autorisation des editions Michel Brûlé, Montréal, Québec, Canada

Translation © 2010 Baraka Books and Robin Philpot

Cover and book design by Folio infographie
Copy editing by Fred A. Reed
Baraka Books
6977, rue Lacroix
Montréal, Québec
H4E 2V4
Telephone: 514-808-8504
info@barakabooks.com
www.barakabooks.com

Avec le soutien financier de la SODEC pour la traduction.

Library and Archives Canada Cataloguing in Publication

Parizeau, Jacques, 1930-

An independent Quebec: the past, the present and the future / Jacques
Parizeau; translated by Robin Philpot.
Translation of: La souveraineté du Québec.

Includes bibliographical references.

ISBN 978-0-9812405-6-5

1. Sovereignty–Economic aspects–Québec (Province). 2. Québec
(Province)–History–Autonomy and independence movements. 3. Québec
(Province)–Politics and government–21st century. 4. Québec
(Province)–Politics and government–1960-.
I. Philpot, Robin II. Title.

FC2926.9.S4P37413 2010   320.1'509714   C2010-902021-9

Legal Deposit, 2nd quarter, 2010
Bibliothèque et archives nationales du Québec
Library and Archives Canada

To the memory of my father
Gérard Parizeau

TABLE OF CONTENTS

system – Supporting the *garde montante* (the rising generation) – Obstacles: income taxes and the public – The importance of decision-making centres – The responsibility of the Caisse de dépôt et placement – The Caisse de dépôt et placement in an independent Quebec

FOREWORD

As I enter my eightieth year and my fortieth year as a sovereigntist, I feel the need to take stock, but not for reasons of nostalgia. Issues facing government still fascinate me today just as they have ever since the Quiet Revolution. Though this is not a memoir, I have delved into my own memories as frankly as possible to help understand today's issues.

I would like to thank the people who helped produce this book. First, Mr. Michel Brûlé, publisher of the original French-language version of this book, who gave me the opportunity to organize my thoughts, and his remarkably efficient assistant publisher, Ms. Marie-Noëlle Gagnon, and copy editor Mr. François Mireault.

For the first time after using its services for many years, I take the opportunity to thank the Parti Québécois Documentation Centre, which has become a formidable instrument under the direction of Mr. Denis Patry and Ms. Lucie Deschênes. The current Director, Ms. Suzanne Turgeon, provided unwavering support, which was particularly vital for Chapter 6.

I deeply appreciate the work of Quebec fiscal expert Professor Luc Godbout and that of Stéphane Gobeil of the Bloc Québécois research team. For several years, Mr. Gobeil has kept me informed about the results of original research conducted anonymously by the Bloc Québécois. The book entitled Pour une gauche efficace by Jean-François Lisée, Director of the Centre d'études et de recherches internationale de l'Université de Montréal, was also extremely helpful.

Serge Guérin, who was my first chief of staff, kindly read the manuscript and suggested corrections and modifications.

I am particularly grateful to Robin Philpot who accompanied me from the beginning, helped in the research, read and discussed each chapter, and revised the manuscript.

Finally, I would like to thank Lisette Lapointe, my wife and my favourite National Assembly Member. She read and meticulously corrected the manuscript, which, however, was but another stage in a long and fruitful collaboration and shared enthusiasm.

I assume full responsibility for the content of this book.

Jacques PARIZEAU, November 2009

Translator's Foreword

It was a great honour to be invited by Mr. Jacques Parizeau in November 2008 to help him with his book project. He did not wish to write a memoir, settle scores with political adversaries, or rehash his speeches made since the 1995 referendum. He was writing a new book addressing the political and economic issues of the day. What an opportunity! Mr. Parizeau has been intimately involved in everything that has happened in Quebec since the 1960s. He has never wavered in his overarching commitment to public service and to the public interest, and has always been respected, even by opponents. As the book progressed, it became obvious that his thoughts, experience, and grasp of issues that face all peoples, nations, and countries in 2010 should be shared with English-speaking readers in Canada and elsewhere. That is when the idea of translating this book was first broached and Mr. Parizeau agreed enthusiastically. Fred A. Reed's contribution to this translation is greatly appreciated. In parallel, Baraka Books had just been founded with a mission to publish "ideas, points of view, and creative works that might otherwise be overlooked because of cultural or linguistic barriers." It is my belief that, with this book, readers will not only see Jacques Parizeau in an entirely different light, but also better understand the cause that he has defended with dignity for forty years.

Robin PHILPOT, May 2010

INTRODUCTION

When I began writing the introduction to this book, French President Nicolas Sarkozy had just reiterated his belief in the unity of Canada and his rejection of an independent Quebec. The leaders of the two sovereigntist parties, the Parti Québécois and the Bloc Québécois, replied in a long letter delivered to the French Embassy in Ottawa and to the France's Consul General in Quebec City. Some might have seen it as the last gasp of a movement, the Parti Québécois, that may have embodied the hopes of a generation, but which after many ups and downs was gradually losing its relevance and, at the same time, its allies. Still, judging by widespread comment and opinion, the impression remains that the more Ottawa and Paris attack the sovereignty movement, the greater the attraction of a sovereign Quebec.

General elections were held in Quebec in 2007 and in 2008 and in Canada in 2008. Following the 2007 election, the Parti Québécois found itself in third place in terms of elected representatives with a popular vote that had fallen to 1973 levels. When the 2008 federal election campaign began many people were questioning the relevance of the Bloc Québécois and its future appeared to be uncertain.

At the end of that eventful year, however, the Parti Québécois regained its status as the Official Opposition and half of all parliamentarians elected in Quebec, whether to Ottawa or Quebec City, were sovereigntists. Furthermore, while the leadership of both parties had begun the year on a note of caution on independence, party activists had successfully reinstated the traditional goal of independence as a key policy plank, just as they had restored the slogan *"On veut un pays"* (*We want a country*). It was much more "can do" approach than the communications "experts" had envisioned. This much was clear: despite forty years of electoral victory and defeat and the heartbreaking, razor-thin loss in the 1995 referendum, when a mere fifty-two thousand votes out of five million decided the outcome, and despite the hesitation of some leaders and the many attempts to sway Quebec public opinion using massive amounts of money, support for the objective and enthusiasm for the ideal of sovereignty appear not only to be surviving, but to be thriving. Even more interesting is that sovereigntists appear to be as politically active as ever. For those who think that the idea of an independent Quebec belonged to a single generation and that it will vanish as that generation passes away, they should note that of the fifty-one Parti Québécois members of the National Assembly, thirty-four, or two thirds, were elected for the first time in 2007 or in 2008. As in the past, however, when the next federal election is called, we can expect to hear calls for the Bloc Québécois to once again justify its existence and the utility of being elected to parliament in Ottawa.

Renewing ideas

Though most of the elected representatives of the sovereignty movement are young, the ideas that drive it have not kept pace. Quite understandably: the Parti Québécois held power in Quebec City for eighteen of the past thirty-two years, which meant that the work of governing a province became the priority. Education and health-care are key policy issues in all societies. In Quebec, however, they became an obsession. The debates, quarrels, and crises that characterized relations between Quebec and Ottawa siphoned off enormous amounts of energy and threw public policy into disarray. Examples abound, but one in particular comes to mind. In 1967 I headed a delegation of Quebec civil servants to the Federal-Provincial Committee on fiscal policy. After months of work, we concluded that, given the unequal division of fiscal resources and the distribution of areas of spending, the federal government found itself systematically "threatened" with surpluses while the provinces toiled with deficits. Discussions about sharing fiscal resources lasted more than thirty years. In 2002 the Séguin Commission created by the Quebec government to investigate fiscal imbalance drew exactly the same conclusion. Nothing had changed, not even the terms of the debate. It was still just as difficult to put together coherent social and economic policies as it had been in 1967.

The 1995 referendum required several years of preparation, which included the groundwork for the administrative structure of an independent country and the development of national policies with clear goals for Quebec. With the referendum loss, that perspective was set aside. In 1996 the new Quebec government focussed on eliminating the deficit just when the federal government began cutting transfer payments to the provinces in an attempt to reduce the federal deficit. Budgetary issues would predominate for years thereafter. The federal government, surely aware of the potential political gains it could make in Quebec, stepped forward to take advantage of Quebec's budgetary cutbacks, quickly providing replacement funding for targeted sectors, such as academics and universities. It also launched a massive public relations and sponsorship campaign that ended in a full-blown scandal and a public inquiry (the Gomery Commission).

For years, thought and reflection about an independent Quebec and how it could be achieved were abandoned. Only the Bloc Québécois, which was not dominated by the concerns of actually holding power, continued to a certain extent to work at breathing new life into the ideas that inspired the movement. And yet renewal is indeed essential. Both pro-sovereignty parties are at the left of centre. Like most progressive parties in Western countries they must rethink their relations with the trade union movement and state capitalism, avoid the extremes of defending acquired rights, or vested interests, which can lead to forms of corporatism, do more to defend the most vulnerable members of society, and adapt to globalization.

Globalization has in fact altered our view of national sovereignty. When suddenly it became clear that an individual could have access to the entire world, that nothing prevented him or her from communicating with others everywhere on the planet, and that even the most powerful governments could not prevent people from linking up with whomever they wished, some came to believe that globalization, through the free exchange of ideas and universal communication, would drastically reduce the role of the state. Certain governments would use their economic and military power to dominate other countries, of course, but their role would gradually diminish and their citizens would meld into the great global family.

The state and globalization

However seductive such notions may have been, things have not turned out that way. It rapidly became clear that not only individuals sitting in front of computers and communicating with the world would feel the impact of globalization. Trade barriers with Asia fell and entire industries disappeared in Western countries. Companies moved production offshore to take advantage of lower wages while those that remained reduced wages to keep up with the competition. People began to realize that the only way to resist these changes and ensure an acceptable future was through education, research, and innovation. They also realized that the idea of working at the same job until retirement was becoming obsolete, that their children might not enjoy the living standards they had, that instability might become endemic, that in terms of education achievement society was being split, and that a new form of social discrimination was emerging and growing. In short, the world was changing very rapidly.

Some thought that the solution was to fight globalization. However, that is like trying to stop the rising tide. The tide cannot be stopped, but dykes, breakwaters and canals can be built to control it and lessen its impact. The question is, who is in charge of building those dykes and canals? In the same vein, someone has to plan and organize school systems, professional training, research, innovation, and protection of the most vulnerable, and to prevent abuse and regulate business. This is a job only the state can do. No other institution throughout history has existed to protect citizens. In the past, the state was represented by feudal lords, then by the king, and by Parliament, but its role has remained unchanged. The responsibility of the state is first and foremost to protect the citizen. In the relationship with the vast, exciting, and sometimes threatening world, the individual working at a computer has only the state to turn to in times of need. These considerations did not exist during the 1995 referendum. For instance, two weeks after I was elected Premier of Quebec in September 1994, my press attaché came running into my office to tell me: "The government is not on Internet." I had recently established a task force to study the possibility of creating an "information highway." But we quickly understood that we had nothing to invent; it already existed and was called the Internet.

On the question of trade liberalization, however, we were further along. As I will explain in Chapter 2, in the late 1980s, the President of the United States proposed a free trade agreement with Canada; the Canadian government agreed in principle. Ontario, the heart of Canada's economy, opposed the free trade agreement and the Ontario government threatened to go to court to prevent the federal government from signing the pact. The Parti Québécois struck an alliance with the Liberal government in Quebec City to make free trade a non-partisan issue, giving Prime Minister Brian Mulroney the necessary political support for the agreement to be adopted. The North America Free Trade Agreement (NAFTA) followed shortly thereafter, creating the conditions for free trade in goods and services across North America. It was only the first stage, albeit the most conventional and best known, of the process that, here and elsewhere, led to globalization. But difficulties soon arose. The demise of the Multilateral Agreement on Investment (MAI) and the crisis over cultural diversity provided two very spectacular signs of societal conflict that turned the spotlight on the role of the state.

We began to realize how powerfully these new international mechanisms could impact the lives of entire peoples, and of the individuals that comprised them. As our awareness grew, we began to grasp the new and powerful role that governments can play in the operations and decision-making of these international mechanisms.

Sovereignty is necessary

Under globalization, national sovereignty has become more, not less important than ever. I have emphasized these ideas for several years in the course of my speaking engagements in universities and colleges throughout Quebec. To other audiences, I have built on my experience as an economist to present some ideas—hopefully clear ones—regarding Quebec's economic development and administration, questions that have been uppermost in my mind for many years. In fact, they explain why I came to support Quebec independence in the first place. During the Quiet Revolution, Quebec gained enough moral authority and financial strength with respect to Ottawa to be able create a pension plan distinct from the Canada Pension Plan and withdraw from twenty-nine shared-cost programs with full fiscal and financial compensation, all in the same year (1964). Although the other provinces could have done the same, they chose not to. A climax came in 1967 when the Quebec government asked to participate in the Franco-German Symphony Project to launch communications satellites into orbit using Russian booster rockets. The initiative came as Canada was concluding an agreement with the United Kingdom and Japan to launch similar satellites with American space boosters...

Quebec could not realistically keep on acting as if it were a distinct country and yet pretend it was still the original country. It was time to choose sides—to choose the country we wanted to belong to. Thus began the combat of a generation. In the beginning, those who led the fight were the same people who for years had struggled against Maurice Duplessis and everything he stood for. That involved many people, from Pierre Elliott Trudeau to René Lévesque, from Father Georges-Henri Lévesque to François-Albert Angers. But those who had fought together against reactionary politics came to a parting of the ways in the 1960s. Some chose Ottawa because they rejected what they called narrow nationalism; they wanted to avoid replacing one sort of reaction by what was considered another variant of the same thing. Others chose Quebec because the Quiet Revolution had revealed a dynamism and an exciting appetite for renewal among the very Quebecers who had been so long scorned.

Political and administrative dysfunction

The struggle between these two groups has left its mark on both contemporary Quebec and Canadian history. Moreover it has led to some bizarre circumstances that are incomprehensible for those not privy to the family secrets. Pierre Elliott Trudeau, for instance, the charismatic Primer Minister of Canada, swept seventy-four of Quebec's seventy-five seats in a general election, while at the same time René Lévesque, the charismatic leader of the Parti Québécois, held power in Quebec. These paradoxical politics at times verged on the absurd. The founding of the Bloc Québécois in Ottawa has effectively clarified the situation. From its inception, the Bloc has steadily obtained significantly more than half of Quebec's seats in the federal parliament, a situation that is now the norm. Yet, when the Bloc Québécois, which runs no candidates outside Quebec, was catapulted into the seats of the Official Opposition in Ottawa as a result of electoral divisions elsewhere, it became clear that the Quebec-Canada paradox was not about to vanish.

Who could doubt that a political dysfunction of this nature inevitably engenders a broader policy and administrative dysfunction? For example, at one point the Quebec government administered thirteen child-support programs while the federal government administered twelve—or perhaps it was thirteen for Ottawa and twelve for Quebec. One federal aid program for the elderly poor was effectively concealed from its would-be beneficiaries who received what they deserved only when a Bloc Québécois MP discovered that many eligible people in his riding were not on the lists, even though they had been on Quebec's welfare rolls a few year earlier. Systematic checking enabled two hundred thousand of Quebec's most vulnerable citizens to register.

Political dysfunction bred dysfunction in public administration. We become so inured to it in the end that we can barely imagine that things could be clear and straightforward. Having been in politics for a long time, I know that, even in the best of circumstances, people can posture, be irrational and demagogical, and stoop to political patronage in order to get reelected. But any politician will ultimately act and speak in accordance with his or her values. One recent example from 2005 comes to mind. It is disappointing, outrageous even, for the government to prolong a university student strike for six weeks to balance the books, on the pretext of reducing the cost of student grant programs by 103 million dollars, only to realize that the federal government would receive seventy of those 103 million dollars under a forgotten federal-provincial agreement. In like manner, to draw up a federal-provincial transfer payment plan so complicated that a provincial finance minister is able to admit, as he introduces an economic recovery program, that he will be losing ten times more in federal transfer payments than expected, is anything but serious.[1] There is no dearth of examples.

The desire for an independent Quebec is not based only on rational arguments, cost and benefit analyses, and hopes of higher living standards. First and foremost comes the desire of a people or a nation to assume full responsibility for itself, to live together and prepare a shared future, and to build on the pride of a shared history. When that people or nation reaches a certain level of well being, however, it hesitates before embarking on what might appear to be an adventure: there may be something to lose. This is why rational, convincing and explicit arguments must be used. Some people get upset at the emphasis sovereigntist leaders put on issues of public administration, but these questions cannot be avoided.

Objections to an independent Quebec have evolved and been refined over time. What they have in common is the economic or administrative dimension, with the emphasis inevitably being placed on old-age pensions. Over the years old-age pensions have been a staple of political debate in nursing homes and hospitals for the chronically ill. "If Quebec separates, you will lose your old-age pensions!" was the mantra hammered into the heads of people who had nothing else to live on.

For years on end it was necessary to calculate and demonstrate, and then, little by little, the fears dissipated. In the 1995 referendum, when sixty-one percent of French-speaking Quebecers, who were the primary targets of the fear campaigns, voted Yes, I began to believe that the fears were in fact fading away. That was consolation for me. For those who see the spectre of ethnicity rise at the sight of the words "French speaker," let me reassure them: the definition used is the same used in public opinion polls, namely those "who speaks French at home."

---

1. Ministère des Finances du Québec, Plan budgétaire 2009-2010, p. G4-G5.

Words matter

Some words about words are in order, and particularly the words *sovereignty, independence* and *separation.* All three mean the same thing. All three mean the country in question has full control over its laws, taxes and the treaties it signs with other countries. Under no circumstances does that mean that the country will never delegate some of its powers to others. However, in order to delegate those powers, it is necessary to have them.

Since the Parti Québécois and the Bloc Québécois were founded they have defined themselves as sovereigntist because that term was less frightening. In the early years, *separatism* was associated with violence and the army, while *independence* was linked to conflict that had so often marked the period of decolonization. *Sovereignty,* and even more so *sovereignty-association,* referred implicitly to negotiation and recognition. Polls clearly confirmed these different perceptions. Today the differences are not as pronounced. We continue saying *sovereignty* out of habit to the point that it is now a trademark. To my mind all three terms mean the same thing and I tend to use them as synonyms. I also know that in France the word *sovereignty* has become conflated with *Euroscepticism,* but that is another story.

The referendums of 1980, 1995 and 201...

The first part of this book examines Quebec's two past bids for sovereignty and what might be involved the next time. The idea is to review how the idea of an independent Quebec emerged and took root, and how it was applied over the past forty years. My purpose is not to write a historical essay, but rather to identify the main issues, starting with those faced by the founding leader René Lévesque, the better to understand how he saw that the goal could be reached. Then comes the way in which his successor—yours truly—saw how Quebec would become a sovereign country. Based on lessons learned from the first attempt led by René Lévesque, I adopted an approach quite distinct from his.

That will bring us to Quebec's third bid for sovereignty, which is still on the drawing board. The conditions have changed so much that a great deal of debate and reflection will be required before the leaders of the Parti Québécois and the Bloc Québécois can decide to go forward, formulate an approach and, after debating it, carry it out. This book will analyse the situation and suggest certain directions and alternatives.

What next? The idea, the Constitution, international relations

The second part of this book examines three questions that I consider to be of crucial importance today. First, how has the idea of sovereignty stood the test of time? Did it belong to one generation, and will it pass away with that generation? Second, where do we stand with respect to the never-ending constitutional debate? The subject has generated a flood of words, and governments have mobilized around it. The Clarity Act was finally hatched, created to present a daunting obstacle to any new attempt by Quebec to become independent, but deafening silence has followed. Where do we go from here? The third question concerns international preparation for the next bid for sovereignty. The Supreme Court referral on a unilateral declaration of sovereignty requires that this issue be addressed.

Is an independent Quebec viable?

The third part of the book has only two chapters. The question is as old as the sovereignty movement itself: is an independent Quebec viable? Although the first chapter addresses traditional accounting issues, i.e., does Quebec send more money to Ottawa than it receives, it also discusses what is nowadays presented as an obstacle to independence, namely the aging of Quebec's population and its indebtedness, factors that would supposedly make sovereignty a risky undertaking.

The second chapter in this section leads us into the fourth and final part of the book, which is resolutely turned toward the future.

How should an independent Quebec be organized and administered? The answer will obviously come from a future constituent assembly. But studies must go forward and hypotheses posited. Should the Quebec Parliament have two chambers—or one? How decentralized should Quebec be once it has taken control of all its resources? Discussion between the government and Quebec's regions and municipalities will only really begin once the referendum has been won. The question is complicated; it deserves attention now.

How will it all work?

The fourth and longest section of the book focusses on the future and reflects the concerns of someone who has been involved in political debate for a long time, and who is also an economist by career and by profession. I will attempt to stick to the fundamental questions, without imagining for an instant that independence will solve all problems. Certain questions that have little to do with formal political arrangements warrant attention simply because they are essential to understanding the current situation. But that will not stop me from indicating where I stand. I've entitled the first chapter of the fourth section (Chapter 9) "The Secret of Growth." Though it may appear to be a catchphrase, this chapter heading represents my view on the subject. Chapter 10 is devoted to the sometimes-adversarial relationship between government and business. Chapters 11 and 12 have the much more ambitious title, "The State and the Citizen." It is impossible to address every issue, but four appear to me to be at the heart of our everyday lives: training, education and work; taxation and distribution of wealth; language; and finally the environment.

The conclusion returns to what I have always considered as the most profound and essential reason for Quebec to become an independent country: for the Quebec people to assume full responsibility for themselves in a democracy in which the state is fully answerable to its citizens.

Chapter 1

PHASE ONE:
NEGOTIATING SOVEREIGNTY-ASSOCIATION

On May 20, 1980, Quebecers were called upon to answer Yes or No to the following question: "The Government of Quebec has made public its proposal to negotiate a new agreement with the rest of Canada, based on the equality of nations; this agreement would enable Quebec to acquire the exclusive power to make its laws, levy its taxes and establish relations abroad—in other words, sovereignty—and at the same time to maintain with Canada an economic association including a common currency; any change in political status resulting from these negotiations will only be implemented with popular approval through another referendum; on these terms, do you give the Government of Quebec the mandate to negotiate the proposed agreement between Quebec and Canada?"

Quebecers were asked to give their government a mandate to negotiate Quebec sovereignty on the basis of pre-established conditions, but they were also assured that once the negotiations were completed the result would be put to another referendum.

Trying independence

The government that proposed this question had been elected on November 15, 1976. The creation of the Parti Québécois, headed by its founder René Lévesque, came about over a long period of time. Since others have described that process in detail I will only review some of the main aspects.

The years that followed World War II were dominated by the Cold War between the United States and the Soviet Union and by a surge of decolonization. With the demise of the former colonial empires, dozens of new countries appeared, with India and Pakistan leading the way in 1947. But it was a sea change, often accompanied by violence, that had little impact in Quebec where a handful of intellectuals were attempting to shake society awake, without much success until the late 1950s. The Quiet Revolution changed everything, inspiring hope among singers, poets, politicians, civil servants, business people and farmers, men and women, young and old. It was in fact a real revolution, a kind of revenge over history that was so well summed up in Jean Lesage's 1962 campaign slogan *Maîtres chez nous* ("Masters in our own house").

That period is known as the Quiet Revolution but, in retrospect, it was not all that quiet. Bombs went off for some years; several people died. The kidnapping of British trade attaché James Cross and of Quebec labour minister Pierre Laporte, the occupation of Quebec by the Canadian army, and the assassination of Pierre Laporte, were the last major acts of violence. But repression did not end the violence. The profound commitment of the Quebec people to democratic values was decisive in the end. During the events of October 1970 René Lévesque played a crucial role in ensuring that his party respected order and democracy.

It should be pointed out however that the violence was relatively marginal when seen in the light of the burgeoning of ideas in *indépendantiste* circles. In 1961 Marcel Chaput published *Pourquoi je suis séparatiste* (*Why I am a separatist*)[1] and Raymond

---

1. Marcel Chaput, *Pourquoi je suis séparatiste*, Montréal, Éditions du jour, 1961, 156 p. In English translation Marcel Chaput, *Why I am a separatist* (translated by Robert A. Taylor), Greenwood Press, Westport, Conn, 1975, 101 p.

Barbeau published *J'ai choisi l'indépendance* (I chose independence).[2] André D'Allemagne and Pierre Bourgault founded the Rassemblement pour l'indépendance nationale (RIN) in September 1960 and Raoul Roy launched *La Revue socialiste* to reach left-wing *indépendantistes*. In 1965, shortly before taking power, the Union nationale under Daniel Johnson published *Égalité ou indépendance*. The 1966 election that brought Daniel Johnson to power was particularly significant historically because for the first time the two pro-independence parties, the RIN and the Ralliement national (RN), ran candidates. The former was a progressive party, while the latter, with roots in the Social Credit movement, leaned to the right. These two parties garnered respectively 5.5 percent and 3.2 percent of votes cast. Most of the support for the RIN and part of the RN's support came from the Liberal Party. Liberal leader Jean Lesage who, as premier, had presided over the Quiet Revolution from its inception was defeated. The party that took power was thus committed either to gaining full equality within Canada or making Quebec an independent nation. Neither was achieved, but the Quiet Revolution continued.

Although the excitement raised hopes, it failed to channel those hopes toward a clearly expressed desire for independence. Many peoples in the world had managed to set up countries for themselves and inevitably the question arose: why not us? Throughout this exhilarating period, the Quebec electorate remained very cautious—some say atavistically so—with regard to a movement that in their eyes lacked credibility. At the same time, Quebecers were thrilled to realize that they too were able to achieve great things when given a chance. The massive Manic-5 hydropower facility north of Baie Comeau became a symbol of technological prowess. The creation of the Caisse de dépôt et placement, Quebec's pension fund, which provided new ways to

---

2. Raymond Barbeau, *J'ai choisi l'indépendance*, Montreal, Éditions de l'Homme, 1961, 127 p.

build on our own resources, was a major advance. Similarly, tripling of the number of secondary school students over a five-year period was a source of pride and hope. It confirmed the adage *Qui s'instruit s'enrichit* ("education is the road to wealth"), spelled out on billboards along Québec's first limited access freeways.

Taking things one step farther, namely leaving Canada, was another question altogether. It meant overcoming fears, be they well founded or fabricated by fear mongers, as well as some very real obstacles. Rhetoric grew shrill, tensions strained relations, and the dysfunction that arises when governments exaggerate in order to win votes combined to make people more and more interested in the idea of independence. But they also had to reconcile their desire for full responsibility for their future with the fear of economic hardship.

The threat of isolation

The threat of being isolated was serious. This requires some explanation. More than half of the goods produced in Quebec were then being exported. The rest of Canada was Quebec's largest external market, with most Quebec-produced goods going to Ontario. Thirty percent of Quebec's industrial workers were concentrated in the textile, garment, shoe and furniture sectors, all of which were protected by customs tariffs and quotas. Although trade barriers gradually dropped following the 1947 General Agreement on Tariffs and Trade (GATT), forerunner of the World Trade Organization (WTO), they still had a long way to fall and in the 1960s remained a formidable obstacle to trade.

Customs duties in the United States were similar to those in Canada, sometimes even higher. The situation prompted André Laurendeau of *Le Devoir* to invite a young Quebec economist by the name of Jacques Parizeau, who was still a federalist, to write an article on the question on November 24, 1961.

The idea of separatism is not necessarily absurd in our economic order, but the obstacles would be numerous and daunting... The province separates from the rest of the country. Suddenly markets in the nine other provinces would be closed and Quebec's industrial production would plummet. Unemployment would grow. Probably more serious is the fact that businesses would only have access to a market of five million people instead of eighteen million, as was previously the case. Foreign capital would leave the province and the standard of living of future generations would be seriously compromised. Montreal would lose its role as the country's leading city. Its port would be the shadow of what it has been... The cost of secession would therefore be high, unless a customs union could be reached with the rest of Canada. Otherwise, Quebec would have three options: an intensive industrialization program, closer relations with Europe or the United States, or, lastly, and for a long time, a drop in standard of living.[3]

If Quebec had declared independence and Canada had replied by treating Quebec as a foreign country, which would have been perfectly normal, and imposed the same customs duties that it levelled on European or American goods, Quebec would have found itself caught between the customs duties imposed by Canada and those imposed by the United States. In short, peoples throughout the world were opting for independence, but if Quebec were to follow suit it would face a major drop in its standard of living.

The solution, as we came to understand several years later, lay in the European Common Market model. The Treaty of Rome that created the Common Market was ratified in 1957, but its relevance for us appeared to be debatable and was, at best, a long way off. In 1968 René Lévesque published *Option Québec*[4] and created the Mouvement Souveraineté-Association. He seized

---

3. Jacques Parizeau, quoted in Jacques Lacoursière, *Histoire populaire du Québec*, tome V: 1960-1970, Sillery, Septentrion, p. 117-118.
4. René Lévesque, *Option Québec*, Montréal, Les Éditions de l'Homme, 1968, 173 p.; *An Option for Quebec*, McClelland and Stewart, 1968, 128 pages.

directly on the problem that had confounded the various independence movements until then. Quebec would become a full-fledged country but it would be associated with Canada under agreements that would provide for free trade between the two. Such agreements would be profitable for both parties. René Lévesque never distrusted the English-speaking world, as often happens among people not familiar with it. Association with English Canada could take different forms and vary in proximity. It would depend on each party's interests. Sovereignty-association as proposed by René Lévesque was largely intuitive, but it corresponded exactly to what Quebecers wanted. It was the ideal middle road between the desire for independence and fear of isolation.

The Mouvement souveraineté-association went on to merge with the Ralliement national (RN) to form the Parti Québécois. Then the Rassemblement pour l'indépendance nationale (RIN) dissolved to allow its members to join the new party. The Parti Québécois was officially founded in 1968 and ran candidates for the first time in the 1970 general election. The campaign started out very strongly, but the opponents of sovereignty organized a major operation to block the movement that became known as the *affaire de la Brink's*. The impact of the operation was so devastating that even forty years later it deserves to be mentioned. On the Sunday morning a week before the vote, half a dozen of the Brink's trucks that normally transported money and securities between banks and financial institutions were parked in front of the Montreal Trust building on Place d'Armes near what was known as St. James Street in Old Montreal. Some twenty armed security guards were loading bags into the trucks when a newspaper photographer happened by (probably on his way from Mass at the Notre-Dame Basilica across the square). The photo was worth thousands of words. Money from Quebec— Quebecers' savings—was heading for Toronto. Hadn't its opponents predicted all along that independence would mean disaster? Nowadays, after decades of debate on money and the economy, the story would not even have made it to the inside pages. In those days, however, people believed that sovereignty was dangerous and that independence would jeopardize the Canadian currency (the *"piastre à Lévesque"* or Lévesque's dollar was an old favourite) and thus imperil old-age pensions and much more. In spite of everything, the Parti Québécois won twenty-three percent of the popular vote and seven seats.

Another general election was held three years later; once again sovereignty-association was the main issue. It was presented perhaps even more radically than in 1970. The question of using the Canadian dollar as the common currency or of a new Quebec currency had yet to be resolved. At the same time, Parti Québécois members had concluded at a party convention held earlier that if they won the election and took power, the new government would have the mandate to achieve sovereignty-association. The party had recovered from the 1970 October Crisis and had regained its strength. A few days before the election, however, the strategy changed. The Parti Québécois would form a government and then two years later it would bring about sovereignty-association, which logically would have entailed holding a referendum, a strategy that would be formally adopted at the 1974 party convention.

The Parti Québécois won thirty-one percent of the popular vote and became the Official Opposition, but had only six seats out of 110. The outcome was perceived as a defeat, paving the way for a two-stage approach that involved gaining power first and then working towards sovereignty, an objective that could only be achieved through a referendum. Many also concluded that sovereignty frightened uncommitted voters. In short, if the emphasis were to be mainly sovereignty, even though it was linked by a hyphen to association with Canada, the likelihood of taking power was slim.

The following general election held in 1976 was prepared with this in mind. The first step was to provide Quebecers with good government and then, during its first term, hold a referendum to obtain the mandate to begin negotiations on achieving the ultimate goal: sovereignty-association. René Lévesque's extraordinary charisma combined with his strong convictions and his innate grasp of what Quebecers felt deep down held together a political party that had been seriously shaken by events, conflicting ideas, and by the sheer magnitude of the campaign funds available to their federalist opponents.

Holding power

The Parti Québécois took power in November 1976, with forty-one percent of the popular vote. The outgoing government had become so estranged from the people that two moribund parties that had not won a single seat in 1973 came back to life as federalists dissatisfied with the Liberals but unable to vote for independence jockeyed for position. Having won the majority of seats, however, the Parti Québécois was now in a position to govern Quebec. René Lévesque's Cabinet was very impressive, undoubtedly the best Quebec had seen in terms of university degrees, career experience and broad public support and acceptance. The quality and breadth of the government's legislative achievements were remarkable, ranging from the Charter of the French Language (Bill 101), through political party financing, agricultural land protection, automobile insurance, to workplace health and safety, and much more. In addition, the instruments created during the Quiet Revolution, combined with transparency in public administration, helped the new government resist the attacks initiated by the financial establishment and won broad support among the general population. The goal of independence was given short shrift however, with the result that preparations for the upcoming referendum suffered. René Lévesque's fundamental intuition, which aimed at maintaining the Canadian economic space, led to some study and research but nothing very systematic. Although reams of paper were produced to evaluate the choice between a Quebec currency and monetary union with Canada, little attention was paid to the budgetary situation of an independent Quebec. The main reason was that government ministers and MNA's were so immersed in the major changes underway in Québec that they neglected the referendum until the question was submitted to the National Assembly at the end of 1979. It was left to René Lévesque to keep the flame of independence burning over and above the demanding requirements of his position.

Preparing for sovereignty-association

The best presentation of sovereignty-association is the White Paper tabled in the Quebec National Assembly on November 1, 1979—three years after the Parti Québécois came to power—entitled *Quebec-Canada: A New Deal. The Quebec Government Proposal of a New Partnership Between Equals: Sovereignty-Association.*[5]

The White Paper put forth a series of well-crafted proposals. The project was based, first of all, on the free circulation of goods, people and capital. There would be a customs union, meaning that customs duties imposed on other countries by Canada and by Quebec would be identical. Quebec wished to establish a monetary union; in other words, Canada and Quebec would use the Canadian dollar. Economic and budgetary policies of both parties would be aligned to meet each other's interests. Quebecers employed by the Canadian civil service were assured of finding similar employment in Quebec's civil service. All Quebec residents who were Canadian citizens would become Quebec citizens and could keep their Canadian citizenship if the Canadian government allowed it. Agreements could be reached regarding a variety of issues such as a common passport or national defence. Quebec would become

---

5. Québec, Gouvernement du Québec, conseil exécutif, 1979, 118 p. *La nouvelle entente Québec-Canada. Proposition du gouvernement du Québec pour une entente d'égal à égal: la souveraineté association.*

a party to the St. Lawrence Seaway agreement, fulfill Canada's obligations under treaties signed and recognize its commitments with respect to the North Atlantic Treaty Organization (NATO) and the North American Aerospace Defense Command (NORAD).

Joint entities such as a currency authority and a tribunal to settle differences in interpretation would be established. Some would have parity representation while others would reflect differences in demographics or economic strength.

At that time in 1979, it was clear that the European experiment had succeeded and that it was continuing to evolve. Other similar associations were appearing on other continents. What had been a flash of intuition in 1967 had proved empirically to be on the mark by 1979. It had also become obvious that it was far easier to form an economic union with politically independent countries than to bring countries that just separated into an economic association. It was inconceivable for Quebec to become independent without entering into an economic association with Canada. No efforts were spared to convince Quebecers that sovereignty and association were essential to Quebec's prosperity and progress. But would Canada agree to such an arrangement? It would be perfectly rational for Canada to do so, since Montreal and Toronto were so intimately linked economically. Canada without Quebec however would still be three times bigger than the newly independent country. Would it be reasonable to think that negotiations could be conducted as though the two parties were on an equal footing and that the entities established under the new association agreement would have complete parity? Quebec could well make such a proposal, but would Canada go along? Tiny Luxemburg could negotiate with Germany as an equal because there were twelve equal countries at the table. It was a different story however when there were only two parties: was it realistic to think that they would be equal?

The White Paper (*Quebec-Canada: A New Deal*) boldly asserted:

Many English-Canadian personalities, politicians and others, tell anyone who will listen that they will categorically refuse to negotiate. This is quite fair, though rather crude. We must not be taken in by it but must, on the contrary, convince ourselves that if the majority of Quebecers say YES in the referendum, Ottawa and the rest of Canada, though they will be disappointed, will have no choice: they will negotiate.

It was a position that became more and more difficult to defend. As time went by, and particularly during the referendum campaign, sovereigntists drew up detailed proposals to which there was little or no response in English Canada, with one remarkable exception. When CBC invited the world-renowned expert on cities, Jane Jacobs, to deliver the Massey Lectures in 1979, she entitled her presentation *Canadian Cities and Sovereignty-Association* and went on to elaborate on her ideas in her book *The Question of Separatism, Quebec and the Struggle over Sovereignty.*[6] The book offered remarkable insight into what the Quebec government was hoping to achieve in 1980 and to Canada's reaction, and still remains relevant to debate in 2010.

But Canada's refusal to negotiate anything hardened into what was close to an official position.

The federal government's arguments had an entirely different thrust. Under a new energy policy the federal government had forced Alberta to sell its oil to Ontario at well below world market prices. The second oil crisis in 1979 caused the price of crude to double in a matter of weeks. In Eastern Canada, oil was imported from Venezuela or the Middle East at world market prices. In order to equalize prices throughout Canada, consumers in the Maritimes and in Quebec received large subsidies. As a result, throughout the referendum campaign, it could quite accurately be said, "If Quebec separates, it will pay more for gas." The federalists were quick to say it, in addition to all the other horror stories about what would happen to a sovereign Quebec.

---

6. Jane Jacobs, *The Question of Separatism, Quebec and the Struggle over Sovereignty,* New York, Random House, 1980, 134 p.

For years sovereigntists had debated the advantages of sovereignty in clear and accessible publications that were as interesting as they were exciting. One book comes to mind, *Quand nous serons vraiment chez nous.*[7] Published by the Parti Québécois Executive Committee in 1972, it became an instant and lasting bestseller. It represented a future based on association with Canada and defended the idea so well among the people of Quebec that, in the minds of many, sovereignty and association were as inseparable as Siamese twins. Elsewhere in Canada, however, the notion of association was a nonstarter; debate was limited to the negative aspects of independence.[8]

The 1980 referendum

Economic issues—the very issues that were most likely to inspire fear among undecided voters—dominated the debate in 1980. The *coup de grâce* came not on the economic front however. A few days before the referendum the Prime Minister of Canada, Pierre Elliott Trudeau, promised solemnly on behalf of his government that if Quebecers voted No a new Constitution would be adopted. Quebecers had been exposed to constitutional demands since they were children and they concluded that the changes announced by the Canadian prime minister would fulfill their aspirations. In fact, the new Constitution that came into force in 1982 took away powers that Quebec had enjoyed since 1791. The people of Quebec had been duped.

On May 20, 1980, forty percent voted yes and sixty percent voted no. René Lévesque was devastated. For many of those who

---

7. Parti Québécois, *Quand nous serons vraiment chez nous*, Montreal, Éditions du Parti Québécois, 1972; (When we are really in our own house).
8. For an excellent study on the conditions and procedures for achieving sovereignty, see the book by Université de Montréal Professor Jacques Brossard, *L'accession à la souveraineté et le cas du Québec, conditions et modalités politico-juridiques*, Presses de l'Université de Montréal, 1976/1995, 853 p. This book remains relevant in 2010.

had followed him, the humiliation left an indelible mark on their lives. Or if it was not humiliation, it was discouragement. One year later, however, in April 1981, the Parti Québécois was reelected with its highest score yet. It seemed that many Quebecers wanted to apologize for the referendum results by reelecting a government whose performance had been outstanding on all fronts. Still, they continued to support Pierre Elliott Trudeau in Ottawa...

A brutal recession began in 1981 and the Quebec economy suffered immensely, but its recovery was surprising, with Quebec getting back on its feet faster than all the other provinces. Corvée-Habitation, a massive home-building and construction industry recovery blitz in which the entire civil society participated, was a stunning example of how effectively Quebec was able use the instruments it had developed. Another demonstration of Quebec's dynamism was the founding of the Fonds de solidarité by the FTQ (Fédération des travailleuses et travailleurs du Québec), Quebec's largest trade union organization. That fund rapidly became the largest venture capital fund in Canada.

On the political front, however, a confusing and trying period had begun. Brian Mulroney's electoral victory in 1984 marked a dramatic change in the attitude of the federal government towards Quebec. The goal was now to bring Quebec back into the Canadian fold. The Constitution of Canada would be modified so that Quebec could adhere to it with "honour and enthusiasm," as the future prime minister said in a speech that went down in history. René Lévesque agreed to take the olive branch in what was described as the *beau risque*, or "beautiful risk." The cabinet and the caucus fell apart. René Lévesque resigned and Pierre-Marc Johnson, the son of the man who had been elected under the slogan of *Equality or Independence*, became premier. *Equality or Independence* was no longer on the agenda, however. Managing the downsizing of an ideal was the order of the day.

Lessons learned

Some important lessons were learned from Quebec's first bid for sovereignty.

1. Sovereigntists had proven that they knew how to administer Quebec. They had undertaken to provide good government; so well did they meet and exceed all expectations that the question would never be raised again. There had been good times and bad, but the Parti Québécois had earned its reputation as a governing party.

2. With the instruments at hand, Quebec was fully able to defend itself against attempts to destabilize it financially. The only impact that had resulted from the closing down of Canadian and American financial markets to Quebec immediately after the 1976 election was to deprive North American brokerage firms of their usual commissions. Borrowing requirements—and they were sizable—were met on the Swiss, British, German and Japanese markets at normal interest rates.

3. It is difficult to act against a refusal to negotiate. It took time to realize that for Canadians, negotiating when no referendum had been held, much less won, would be a kind of betrayal. It was like admitting in advance that the sovereigntists were going to win.

4. By the same token, those who considered themselves Canadian would not be satisfied with economic and financial arguments in defence of their country. Sovereigntists had inevitably spent too much time on economic arguments and justifications, mainly because fears about Quebec independence focussed on those issues. For Canadians, the idea that their country was threatened prompted them to turn to arguments of national pride and emotion. It was as if they were at war. That mindset explains episodes like the "night of the long knives" (*la nuit des longs couteaux*) in 1981 when Canada's first ministers conspired—the term is accurate—to amend the Constitution of Canada behind René Lévesque's back, without even informing

him of the commitments made that night. Ever since, Quebec has never ratified the new Constitution, be it under a Liberal or a Parti Québécois government.

5. Finally, in the atmosphere of perpetual confrontation between Quebec and Ottawa and between federalist and sovereigntist parties, the charisma of the premier of Quebec is crucial to ensure lasting cohesion. René Lévesque had what was required. In the next round, Lucien Bouchard was able to play a similar vital role.

Chapter 2

PHASE 2:
ACHIEVING SOVEREIGNTY

On October 30, 1995, Quebecers were asked to answer Yes or No to the following question: "Do you agree that Québec should become sovereign after having made a formal offer to Canada for a new economic and political partnership within the scope of the bill respecting the future of Quebec and of the agreement signed on June 12, 1995?"

The result of the 1995 referendum was the same as in 1980. The No side won, but, this time, by the narrowest of margins. A mere fifty-two thousand votes out of the five million votes cast separated the two camps. The Yes side had obtained 49.4 percent. The outcome was clearly much better than in 1980, in terms of both support and content.

The wording of the question reflected a fundamental change in how people perceived that sovereignty would be achieved. In 1980, Quebecers were asked to authorize their government to negotiate. No action would be taken to make Quebec independent before a second referendum that would ratify the results of negotiations. In 1995, Quebecers were asked to authorize their government to achieve sovereignty. Negotiations would be conducted with the federal government, but if they were not completed within a specified time, the Quebec National Assembly would have the power to declare Quebec an independent country. Precautions were taken to ensure that negotiations would be conducted in good faith. A bill defined in clear and simple terms the road map to sovereignty and the transition measures. That bill was delivered to all homes in Quebec. If the Yes option won, the outcome would be independence. It was a completely different operation than in 1980.

More and more countries

In the fifteen years between the two referendums, major changes had occurred in the world, in the way North Americans perceived those changes, and in relations between Canada and Quebec. The world was not seen in the same light. René Lévesque's remarkable intuition, which had kept him from going too far too fast, was no longer relevant. What had been far away was now close at hand. What had been seen as moving too fast then could now be considered as much less risky.

The changes that had occurred were in fact breathtaking. Everywhere, existing political structures began to crumble. It was extraordinary to witness the implosion of the Soviet block almost overnight. Perhaps more surprising was the fact that, with the exception of the Caucasus, very little violence ensued. Who could have imagined that Russia would agree so calmly to the independence of the Ukraine after centuries of domination? The break up of Yugoslavia into seven countries was more dramatic, especially where Serbia was involved. On the other hand Czechoslovakia split into two separate countries with no violence, based simply on decisions made by the two parliaments. Assets were divided up just as couples handle divorces, by mutual consent.

The most interesting aspect of these movements was that the newly created countries expressed the desire of each people, and of each nation as defined by history, to achieve political autonomy.

In Western Europe's democracies, where the nation-state had long kept internal cultural differences at the folklore level, problems of identity became so serious that the unity of several of these countries was seriously called into question. It was no longer farfetched to imagine the Flemish and the Walloons dividing Belgium into two countries once the status of Brussels had been settled. Scotland regained the parliament that it had lost three centuries before and a pro-independence party now holds power. The Catalan people might already have been independent if economic development had not attracted large numbers of Spaniards from poorer regions to settle in Catalonia. The Basques were to hold a referendum on independence in 2008—until the central parliament in Madrid prohibited it. In other countries, centrifugal forces are growing, although they are not necessarily threatening the unity of the state, Bavaria in Germany being a case in point.

Small countries with large markets

Europe has become a kind of laboratory where all forms of political organization are not only mooted but put into practice. These include independence in the traditional sense; federalism combined with cultural independence (e.g., the radical decentralization of the Belgian radio and television network); attempts to establish direct relations with the European Union while maintaining the traditional nation-state structure; a Europe of regions; or a Europe of large cities. This remarkable ferment can only exist when it is understood that each people or each nation has the right to define the political status that corresponds to their respective aspirations, but on the fundamental condition that the people or the nation belong to a large market. In short, at the end of the twentieth century Europe has taught the world that no country is too small to develop as long as it is part of larger trade zone or market. The country's prosperity in the larger market will depend on its attention to increasing and improving the productivity and innovation of its businesses.

The discovery was nothing less than a revolution. Previous to it, a country's political boundaries had economic meaning in that they often defined the market. Inversely, countries could come to exist as a result of economic decisions. German unification in the second half of the nineteenth century, for instance, resulted from a customs union known as the Zollverein. Canada too was an economic creation made up of two principal elements: the construction of a transcontinental railroad and the establishment of customs duties that favoured the east-west circulation of goods by rail, as opposed to a more normal and natural north-south exchange. Actions designed to create a market also created a country. In Canadian economic history textbooks they are known as the *National Policy*.

Large markets exist throughout the world today. The European Union is obviously the grandfather and a model for others. The North American Free Trade Agreement (NAFTA) was seen by some as a first step towards free trade in the Americas. When the Mercosur or Southern Common Market in South America developed around Brazil, the United States realized that a free trade zone for the Americas had no future. The West African Economic and Monetary Union (UEMOA) enabled some of the world's poorest countries to present a united front to the large economic powers. The same can be said about the Caribbean Community and Common Market or CARICOM.

It took time to understand what the European Union meant and to draw political conclusions. When the Secretary General of the United Nations stated in Montreal in 1995 that he would not be surprised if the UN comprised two hundred member countries by the year 2000, some believed (or pretended to believe) that he was exaggerating. No country is too small to prosper. Economic integration does not reduce the number of independent countries, but increases them. From that point of view, the idea of a people wishing to establish a country of its own is neither backwards nor outdated. It is very much in step with history.

All of this goes to explain how the context had changed when the 1995 referendum was held.

Free trade between Canada and the United States

In 1988, the United States Congress had become very protectionist. Members of Congress and senators were regularly introducing bills to protect local industry. Although I have never seen a complete list, I did see enough to realize the potential danger for the Canadian and Quebec economies. President Reagan, who had already proposed a free trade agreement with Canada a few years earlier, reiterated his proposal. A trade war between the United States and its number one customer, Canada, had to be avoided. Prime Minister Mulroney seized the opportunity—he too was aware of the danger of the bills before Congress. Western Canada agreed since it had traditionally favoured free trade with the United States. In Ontario, the picture was completely different. Since the *National Policy* was adopted in 1878, American companies had established branch plants in southern and southwestern Ontario, the centre of Canada. These plants became the industrial heart of the country. Enjoying tariff protection, Canadian companies also prospered, but periodic waves of mergers and acquisitions reinforced the domination of American companies, particularly in the manufacturing sector.[1] Would a free trade agreement hasten the departure of American branch plants from Canada? Ontario Premier David Peterson did not believe he could run that risk. He even threatened to take the prime minister of Canada to court to prevent him from signing the free trade agreement. Although that threat never materialized, Premier Peterson led an intensive campaign against free trade.

Quebec therefore held the trump card. Quebec Premier Robert Bourassa leaned toward free trade but feared the reaction of the union movement. The leader of the Official Opposition in Quebec at the time was generally opposed, a position consistent with traditional Parti Québécois thinking. Some leaders of the

---

1. The 1950s became known as *The Big Takeover.*

Parti Québécois were not so hesitant, particularly Bernard Landry.[2] At that time, I had left politics after being finance minister for eight years and had returned to teaching economics at HEC Montréal, Quebec's leading business school. In this capacity, before being elected to head the Parti Québécois, I had defended the free trade agreement before a parliamentary committee of the Quebec National Assembly. The free trade debate and its impact are fundamental to understanding the 1995 referendum. It started in 1988 and culminated seven years later in 1995. Since the strategy was mine, as was the responsibility for implementing all but one element of it, this part of the text is written directly in the first person with no attempts to hide responsibility.

There was no political debate about the free trade agreement in Quebec because Robert Bourassa and I did not want one. We chose to address it as a bi-partisan issue. From an economic standpoint, that approach was understandable. American branch plants played less of a role in the Quebec economy than they did in Ontario. Furthermore, Quebec companies, many of which had thrived because of the Quebec Stock Saving Plan, envisioned rapid expansion in the United States if trade barriers were eliminated. The 1982 recession had left its mark, but the new class of entrepreneurs, or the *garde montante*, demonstrated a new dynamism and had gained a certain moral authority never seen before in Quebec business circles.

The unions were generally opposed to free trade on principle. The Mulroney government had however paid particular attention to transition measures for workers who might be affected by free trade. On the other hand, Quebec's industrial unions quickly realized that their interests did not coincide with those of the fellow trade unionists in Ontario. The position taken by the Quebec Steelworkers was particularly significant.

---

2. Bernard Landry, *Commerce sans frontières: le sens du libre-échange*, Québec-Amérique, 1987, 189 p.

The American protector

The Liberal Party and the Parti Québécois agreed on the objective, but for different reasons. Both parties understood the advantages of free trade for Quebec businesses, but our political motivation was very different. For years English Canada had been threatening Quebecers with devastating sanctions if they were to opt for independence. Canada, they said, would stop purchasing clothes, textiles, shoes and furniture from Quebec, all industries that still played a relatively important role in Quebec's industrial structure. Some people even threatened to refuse selling western beef to Quebec—one wonders whether western cattle raisers had been consulted. If these threats were carried out, of course, Quebec's unemployment would rise and its standard of living would drop.

The situation was clearly not the same as it had been in 1968 when René Lévesque published *Option Québec*. Nevertheless, after for so many years of hearing about the perils of independence if Canada did not cooperate on trade, people had a hard time understanding the complete reversal of the situation that free trade with the United States would bring about. An agreement of that nature is governed by rules. Relations between businesses would be subjected to well-defined rules that political conflicts could not undo easily. For example, in 1974 in an attempt to reserve the Ontario market for oil from Alberta, the federal government prohibited oil refined in Quebec from entering Ontario (the Borden Line), thus effectively shutting down half of Montreal's refining facilities and jeopardizing Montreal's entire petrochemical industry. Quebec was handcuffed. Arbitrary decisions of that kind by the federal government would be unthinkable within the framework of the free-trade agreement. Ottawa could no longer invent a "new border" for the international oil trade. In fact, the United States was unintentionally becoming the protector of Quebec's interests as Quebec dealt with mood swings in English Canada.

In the event of sovereignty, Quebec still had to ensure that Canada would not be in a position to exclude it from a two-party agreement. Standing alone and facing Canada, Quebec would have to deal with emotional, political and sometimes irrational issues generated by the weight of history. In addition, companies would likely want to keep their business in order during what would appear to Canadians as an unacceptable change. Would the rationality of business or emotion, combined inevitably with demagoguery, prevail?

The arrival of the United States changed everything. The Americans would become the guarantors of a smoothly operating, integrated North American market, to be quickly reinforced upon ratification of the free trade agreement; the flow of trade would change dramatically. Quebec's exports to the United States increased at an average of eight percent a year during the 1990s, whereas annual exports to the rest of Canada increased by less than one percent.

When President Clinton, speaking in 1993 in Miami, proposed a free trade zone of the Americas stretching from Tierra del Fuego to the North Pole, nobody suggested that Quebec could be excluded. Exclusion of Cuba could have been envisioned as long as Castro remained in power, but not Quebec. Quebec's trade with the United States already represented the equivalent of trade between that country and Brazil and Argentine combined.

In the months leading up to the 1995 referendum, James Blanchard, United States Ambassador to Canada, regularly reminded people that Quebec would not automatically become a member of the North American Free Trade Agreement or NAFTA.[3] That was true of course since NAFTA is a tripartite accord. Several articles would have to be amended to include a fourth party. In most cases, it would be a simple case of establishing consistency. One provision could be problematic: the

---

3. James Blanchard, *Behind the Embassy Doors, Canada, Clinton and Quebec*, Toronto, McClelland & Stewart, 1998, 300 p.

parties to NAFTA agreed that if other countries wished to join, the three founders could set conditions for their entry. The context implies that these conditions are economic by nature. For instance, the founding countries would not want a Marxist country to join NAFTA. The provision was written in a manner that might allow Canada to attempt to impose political obligations on an independent Quebec, such as official bilingualism. For this reason, in its relations with the United States, Quebec strives to emphasize shared democratic values, respect of human rights and the rule of law. Efforts must be made to ensure that Canada cannot use fundamental political considerations to hamper Quebec within NAFTA. From an economic standpoint, however, the manner in which Quebec practices capitalism has never been a problem despite what some people have claimed.

By 1995 it had become clear that Quebec's economic future lay in its relations with the United States, especially as the North American economy became steadily more integrated. Canada obviously had a political existence, but as an economic entity, it came to resemble a dead end for Quebec. Association between Quebec and Canada, which had been essential in 1967, became much less important under the North American Free Trade Agreement. That is the economist's point of view, but the politician has to see things in an entirely different light.

Partnership

Over the years, the idea of sovereignty-association had become so dominant that it was almost impossible to shake. The change would have been too abrupt. The fact is that I was unable to convince people that it was an anachronism we no longer needed. For sovereigntists to maintain their unity, some form of an offer to Canada was essential. The Agreement of June 12, 1995 reached by the Parti Québécois, the Bloc Québécois and the Action démocratique du Québec offered Canada an economic and political partnership that would be the basis for negotiations between Quebec and Canada after a Yes vote in the referendum. This approach was forced upon me during a convention of the Bloc Québécois. But I based my strategy nonetheless entirely on the notion that a refusal by Canada to negotiate would not stop Quebec from moving forward. We would negotiate, of course, but the other party's refusal to do so would not prevent us from achieving our objective. I am convinced that it was the healthiest approach, but it might have been too simple and straightforward, and not "political" enough. And it definitely reflected the Quebec mentality of giving Canada "one last chance."

Thus the three parties drafted the economic and political agreement to be presented to Canada. Since I was the least credible of all possible negotiators, I had included in the bill on Quebec's future a provision for a negotiations monitoring committee independent of the government. Representatives of the opposition would be invited to take part in this committee mandated to monitor negotiations and report to the National Assembly. If, during the ensuing year, the committee concluded that negotiations had ended in an impasse or had stalled, the National Assembly would have the power to declare independence. With these conditions in place, Quebec could propose a partnership with Canada without fear that English Canada's refusal would in reality be a thinly disguised veto, as it had been during the 1980 referendum campaign.

The Canadian dollar

The same idea guided us on the question of a future currency. Were an independent Quebec to choose the Canadian dollar as its currency, nobody could stop it from doing so. It would obviously be preferable for Quebec to have representatives on the board of the Bank of Canada and participate in establishing monetary policy, but if the divorce turned bitter, Canada could not prevent Quebec from continuing to use the Canadian dollar.

The dollars that Quebecers hold in their bank accounts could not be taken away. The system is as it is: the Bank of Canada could in no way lessen credit in Quebec without lessening it everywhere else. Far-reaching technical studies were conducted to determine under what conditions Quebecers could be prevented from using the Canadian dollar. Such an outcome would have been possible only by imposing a multitude of controls. One of the least drastic among them would be to prohibit Canadians from using their credit cards in other countries—hardly a way to win friends and influence people. In short, Quebecers could not be prevented from keeping the Canadian dollar if they so chose. My mind was made up: we would keep it.

But why? In the 1990s a great many monetary instruments were concocted. Short-term movement of international capital increased exponentially. At times or on specific days, the movement of Canadian dollars would represent thirty or forty times the value of commercial trade leading to extremely volatile exchange rates. Creating a new currency in that context meant taking an enormous risk. Since the climate could be expected to be hostile, a new currency could be demolished within days. It was much better to declare that the Canadian dollar would be maintained. In such a case, the Bank of Canada would have been responsible for stabilizing the dollar in the days following the referendum and after a unilateral declaration of independence in case negotiations failed. In Quebec, the Caisse de depot et placement would coordinate the stabilization of Quebec Government and Hydro-Québec bonds.[4]

The French-speaking population has to decide

The entire referendum strategy was based on the notion that negotiations with Canada, which were inevitable on some issues and desirable on others, had to be conducted under conditions

---

4. This became known as the "Plan O."

in which Canada was not in a position to refuse to negotiate, and in so doing, prevent Quebecers from achieving sovereignty if that was what they wished. It was vital to avoid depending on Canada's good will, since that good will would only be present if Quebec did not depend on it. Negotiations would only be successful if it was clear that their failure would not prevent Quebec from becoming independent.

It was also necessary to avoid what minorities might perceive as pettiness or, worse, as an act of revenge on history. I have always thought, and continue to think, that it is necessary to rely on the French-speaking population to achieve independence. Let me make it very clear that "French-speaking population" does not mean those of French Canadian descent, but all those of whatever origin who live their lives in French. That does not mean that other Quebecers are adversaries. Nonetheless, the decades-long campaign against Quebec independence supported in 1995 by organizations such as the Jewish, Greek, and Italian Congresses in Quebec, introduced an ethnic dimension into political debate that poisoned the atmosphere. For example, where McGill University levelled quotas on Jewish students for many years, and its Board of Governors, the boards of the Canadian chartered banks, and English private clubs barred Jews as a matter of policy, a few lines written by Lionel Groulx were enough to tar him and, at the same stroke, all French-speaking Quebecers, with the brush of anti-Semitism. Everybody conveniently forgot that Trois-Rivières was the first place in the British Empire to elect a Jew to parliament.

The debate on Quebec's future produced some memorable moments. The time when the Association of Polish Second World War Veterans claimed before the Bélanger-Campeau Commission hearings on Quebec's future that Quebecers had no right to have their own country remains to this day one of the most comical moments of my political career. Just when you think you've heard it all before, then somebody comes along and surprises you with their foolishness.

Two important questions remained to be clarified, the status of Quebec's English-speaking population and that of the Aboriginal peoples in an independent Quebec. If the National Assembly were to make a unilateral declaration of independence after negotiations failed, international opinion would have to be reassured on these two issues. Quebec was well positioned to succeed.

Few people could question the fact that, as a minority, Quebec's English-speaking population had always enjoyed not only excellent conditions, but also constitutional protection. Some of the English-speaking minority's political and economic powers had diminished as a result of the Quiet Revolution; the French Language Charter had laid the groundwork for a society that would operate in French, even though the Supreme Court had rolled back many important provisions. With the referendum approaching, it was important to be clear about what the position of the government of an independent Quebec would be. A White Paper was published that met the demands of the English-speaking community, with one exception: English schools would be unable to maintain their enrollment by recruiting immigrant children. The White Paper was deigned to stand the test in any international forum.

As most English-speaking Quebecers undoubtedly desired to remain Canadians if Quebec were to become an independent country, they would, as Canadian residents of Quebec, automatically receive Quebec citizenship. An independent Quebec would also recognize dual citizenship. Thus a Quebec citizen who wished to remain a Canadian citizen could simply turn to Ottawa to settle the matter. Citizenship thus became a Canadian issue rather than a Quebec issue and on the international scene if there were to be a villain it would not be Quebec.

Negotiations with Aboriginal peoples

The Aboriginal question was more delicate. In 1975, the Bourassa Government signed the James Bay and Northern Quebec

Agreement with the Inuit and the Cree, which was later expanded to include the Naskapis. That landmark agreement established the framework of Aboriginal rights with respect to the development of a huge territory reaching from the Abitibi region to Ungava Bay. Under the agreement, the Aboriginal signatories abandoned all their land claims.[5] Federal and Quebec legislation later confirmed the agreement.

The Parti Québécois took power the following year, and promptly transformed what was essentially a contract for economic development of the Far North into a finely tuned political document.

René Lévesque addressed the Aboriginal question in a completely new way. By recognizing eleven distinct Aboriginal nations and defining the conditions for creation of Aboriginal governments in 1983 and 1985, René Lévesque established a framework for future negotiations; these would be difficult, and complex. Historical wrongs cannot be righted overnight, even with a treasure trove of good will and good intentions.

When I became premier of Quebec in 1994, I kept responsibility for the Aboriginal affairs secretariat, knowing that it was of utmost importance. Among the talks then in progress, those with the Innu in northeastern Quebec appeared to be closest to completion. The federal Indian Act recognizes nine Innu First Nations. Under Quebec law, the Innu form a single nation. The three Atikamekw communities were also included in negotiations alongside the Innu. An agreement was imminent, and so was the referendum. The Innu chose to suspend negotiations and wait to see the results of the referendum. Negotiations resumed years later, but with only four Innu First Nations, since the Innu Nation recognized by Quebec, which included all nine communities, had broken down. The new round of negotiations continues, illustrating once again that patience is a necessary ingredient for success.

---

5. Section 2.1 of the James Bay and Northern Quebec Agreement.

Debate with the James Bay Cree nation had the potential to create serious problems for Quebec on the international scene. Focus was on the hydroelectric development of the Great Whale River. The Cree denounced the project that would have flooded large tracts of land over which they claimed to hold rights. Moreover, they demanded compensation under the James Bay Agreement, and the amounts increased each time Hydro-Québec modified the project. Supported by the Canadian Department of Foreign Affairs, the Cree took their cause to major cities in the United States and Europe. In certain universities in the United States, they mobilized to boycott and divest of Hydro-Quebec bonds. To a certain degree, the campaign succeeded. It made Quebec look bad; I became increasingly convinced that Quebec could do without the Great Whale project altogether. So I gave instructions to cancel the project and everything calmed down. Fourteen years later, no Quebec government has re-launched the Great Whale project even though several other major hydro facilities have been brought on line or announced.

The Aboriginal question will always require serious attention from Quebecers who wish to establish an independent Quebec. How Quebec handles administration of Aboriginal affairs will be a criterion used internationally to determine how well an independent Quebec can manage its own affairs.

International recognition

Preparing the international dimension of the referendum was obviously much more extensive than this overview allows. On the international front, just like on the domestic front, it was imperative for the federal government to know that its refusal to cooperate would not prevent us from moving ahead. There was no other way to reach our goal. If negotiations stalled and the National Assembly declared Quebec an independent country, the declaration had to have an impact. In other words, Quebec had to be recognized. Such recognition would logically come from the United States, but it was totally unrealistic to expect Washington to act. It would have been enough of a challenge for the Americans to inform English Canadians, whom they consider as part of the family, that Quebec could not be expelled from NAFTA following a democratic vote for sovereignty. It would have been too much to ask for them to be the first to recognize Quebec. Recognition by France thus became the cornerstone or our international strategy. It was a very complicated task that took years, from 1988 through to the 1995 referendum.

On the Larry King show on CNN on Monday, October 23, 1995 then-French President Jacques Chirac came out in clear support of the recognition of Quebec following a majority Yes vote in the referendum. At the same time, the government of Canada was pressuring the White House to obtain clear presidential support for a united Canada. President Bill Clinton responded to Canada's demand but was surprisingly moderate in his remarks.[6] We knew that it would be difficult for the United States government to stand by while France and other members of the French-speaking world helped bring into being a new country in the Americas without it.[7]

In a nutshell, if a majority of Quebecers voted Yes and if Paris moved quickly according to a well-established plan, Quebec had everything it needed to initiate talks with the United States.

Territorial integrity: behind the scenes

Before concluding the chapter on the 1995 referendum we should describe the studies that were carried out on the budgetary, financial, legal, and administrative consequences of Quebec independence.

---

6. "This vote is a Canadian internal issue for the Canadian people to decide. And I would not presume to intervene with that..." See Appendix I for the statements made by Jacques Chirac and Bill Clinton on the eve of the referendum.

7. A detailed presentation of this question can be found in Jacques Parizeau, *Pour un Québec souverain*, Montreal, VLB éditeur, 1997, pp. 283-289.

As noted earlier, although some studies were conducted in the run-up to the 1980 referendum, only a very few were sufficiently detailed. However, during the period that began with the Bélanger-Campeau Commission in 1990 following the demise of the Meech Lake Accord, many in-depth studies were generated.[8] First came those conducted by the Commission Secretariat, and then another set of studies requested by the Parliamentary Committee created under Act 150, mandated to examine the consequences of sovereignty. Then in 1994 and 1995, further studies were performed under the direction of the Quebec minister in charge of restructuring. In addition to examining the impact of sovereignty, they suggested how government would be organized following a declaration of independence.

Some of these studies were to play a vital role. For instance, the drafting of the budget of an independent Quebec and the rules governing the sharing of assets and debt established by the Secretariat of the Bélanger-Campeau Commission formed the basis for later studies, specifically those conducted by Claude Lamonde[9] in 1995, which remain to this day the very best work done on the subject.[10]

Most of the studies carried out for the Parliamentary Committee were unsolicited. But the Secretariat published all the studies in juxtaposition. Many intended to show that independence would lead straight to the apocalypse. However, one of them, commissioned by the Secretariat, was particularly relevant and continues to be so. Entitled *The territorial integrity of Quebec in the event of the attainment of sovereignty*,[11] it touched

---

8. See Chapter 5 for more on this post-Meech Commission.

9. Commission d'étude des questions afférentes à l'accession du Québec à la souveraineté; Claude Lamonde, *Les enjeux et la problématique du partage des actifs dans le cadre du partage de la dette advenant la souveraineté*, vol. 4, p. 757-780.

10. Please see Chapter 7 for more détails.

11. Thomas M. Franck, Rosalyn Higgins, Alain Pellet, Malcom N. Shaw, Christian Tomuschat, *L'intégrité territoriale du Québec dans l'hypothèse de l'accession à la souveraineté*, in *Exposés et études volume 1, Les attributs d'un*

on a fundamental issue. The terms set by the International Commission set up to examine the question were as follows:

1. Assuming that Quebec were to attain sovereignty, would the boundaries of a sovereign Quebec remain the same as its present boundaries, including the territories attributed to Quebec under the federal legislation of 1898 and 1912, or would they be those of the Province of Quebec at the time of the creation of the Canadian Federation in 1867?

2. Assuming that Quebec were to attain sovereignty, would international law enforce the principle of territorial integrity (or *uti possedetis*) over any claims to dismember the territory of Quebec, and more particularly:

   a) the claims of the Natives of Quebec invoking the right to self-determination within the meaning of international law;

   b) the claims of the Anglophone minority, particularly in respect of those regions of Quebec in which this minority is concentrated;

   c) the claims of the inhabitants of certain border regions of Quebec, regardless of ethnic origin?

The document was to provide a response to Pierre Elliott Trudeau's mantra—dear to federalists—that "If Canada is divisible, then so is Quebec."

A committee of legal experts was set up to study the question. It included Thomas M. Franck, Becker Professor, School of Law, Director, Center of International Studies, New York University; Rosalyn Higgins, Q.C., Professor, London School of Economics, member of the Human Rights Commission; Alain Pellet, Professor of Public Law at the University of Paris X—Nanterre and at the Paris *Institut d'Études politiques*, member of the Inter-

Québec souverain, Commission d'étude des questions afférentes à l'accession du Québec à la souveraineté, Assemblée nationale du Québec, mars 1992. (*The territorial integrity of Quebec in the event of the attainment of sovereignty,* translated from the French by William Boulet, revised by J. Maurice Arbour, Professor, Faculty of Law, Université Laval.)

national Law Commission of the United Nations, Malcolm N. Shaw, Professor, Faculty of Law, University of Leicester; and Christian Tomusschat, Professor, Institut für Völkerrecht, Bonn University, President of the International Law Commission of the United Nations.

The unanimous conclusion took the form of a clear-cut legal opinion: An independent Quebec would maintain its current boundaries.

Throughout 1995, as mentioned above, we conducted systematic budgetary and financial studies focusing on how the federal government debt and assets would be shared, how revenue and spending would be divided, and on the impact of the elimination of overlapping programs. We also studied how the newly independent state would be organized administratively, including public security and the armed forces. Debate continued on how the United States would react to a declaration of sovereignty, which led to a study of the principles the United States government applies to existing treaties when a country is divided. Rogers and Wells, a leading Washington law firm, conducted the study, William Rogers being a former Secretary of State. The conclusion was likewise clear-cut. The United States would respect the commitments made to the parties on all points covered. If amendments were in order, the normal notifications and processes applying to treaty renegotiation would be followed. There would be no breach in application.

Conclusion

To conclude, the 1995 strategy was devised to reassure Quebecers that the project presented to them was realistic and that they would have control over the final outcome. That meant that we could allay the fears that had so influenced the results of the 1980 referendum. The strategy was extremely effective among the French-speaking population. Overall in Quebec, sixty-one percent voted Yes while, on the island of Montreal, sixty-eight percent of French-speaking voters supported Quebec sovereignty. Voter turnout was nothing less than phenomenal, with ninety-four percent of those registered casting their votes. The No side squeaked by nonetheless. Over time, the legitimacy of the result was seriously called into question. Since I am too concerned personally, it is not up to me to comment on Robin Philpot's analysis and revelations in his book *Le referendum vole* (The Stolen Referendum).[12] I can only invite people to read it... Quebecers were deprived of an extraordinary opportunity to have their own country.

I resigned as premier early in 1996 and was replaced by Lucien Bouchard who had played a key role during the referendum campaign and was immensely popular. Quebec then began a long period dominated by the goal of attaining a zero deficit while the goal of sovereignty was gradually pushed onto the back burner, as had happened after the 1980 referendum. The second attempt to achieve sovereignty was over.

---

12. *Le referendum volé*, Montreal, Les Intouchables, 2005, 208 p.

Chapter 3

GLOBALIZATION AND PROTECTING CITIZENS

Quebec's third attempt to become an independent country will be dominated by the context of growth and entrenchment of globalization. At first glance one might be tempted to think that the role of the nation-state diminishes under globalization. Once again, using new arguments but with the same old objectives, attempts will be made to prevent nations that are not yet independent from becoming so. The bulldozer of globalization will leave, it will be said, no room for the nation-state, or more pointedly for nation-states that are supposedly too small or too weak to play in the major leagues.

I believe the contrary, namely that globalization makes the nation-state's traditional role more essential than ever. Confronted with the dangers, excesses, and abuse brought on by globalization, despite its undeniable advantages, the citizen's ultimate protector can only be the state. He or she can only influence that protector in a democracy. No matter how small a nation state, it cannot be prevented from enacting its own laws and administering its own affairs. Governments can be corrupted or blackmailed; citizens can be frightened, but nobody can take away the state's right to legislate. Between the individual in front of a computer screen and the great wide world, there exists an intermediary, an identity, a framework, a sense of belonging, namely the tribe, the people or the nation, and the civil authority that represents it.

Clearly the role of the nation-state in this new world is increasingly different from the one we have been accustomed to. It will take time to find our bearings. To use concrete examples, politicians and citizens have difficulty grasping that the price of milk or eggs in Quebec today is not established in Quebec City, nor in Ottawa, but rather in Geneva. If the government of Quebec hopes to protect Quebec farmers, it will have to get to Geneva sooner or later.

Quebec will make a third bid for independence. The strategy and the tactics remain to be defined. The years following the 1995 referendum were so dominated by hesitation, diversion, and internal debate that it became very difficult to adapt to the changes that were brutally impacting the whole world. Another chapter reviews the political evolution of the sovereignty movement during those years and the strategic alternatives that are available to us today. But first, let us describe globalization and its impact on the powers of governments, then explain why globalization does not dilute the sovereignty of nation-states, but rather makes it even more necessary than ever.

The new world of communications

First let us define our terms. Globalization has become a kind of catchall that means different things to different people. For me, it consists of two main elements: communications and free trade.

The impact of instantaneous communication and universal dissemination of information and knowledge via new information technologies has been widely discussed. It is a new industrial revolution, one that has influenced the lives of individuals more than anything else since the invention of the printing press in the fifteenth century. This is all well known and understood, but it is still amazing to see that this revolution owes so much of its vitality to young people and the games they play.

Sometimes we lose sight of the fact that new information technologies gave rise to an explosion in the creation and multiplication of methods of payment and credit. Combined with instant and theoretically unlimited transmission, this liquidity explosion makes it possible for a few companies—or even a single individual—to speculate and jeopardize the exchange rate of an entire currency. The Long Term Capital Management failure is a case in point. Using mathematical models, LTCM forced the devaluation of several Asian currencies in 1997, which in turn provoked a succession of acute commercial credit crises. Between 1994 and 1998, LTCM's operations took a turn for the worse. In 1998, faced with imminent bankruptcy that could have led to a "fire sale" of ninety billion dollars of securities on the financial markets, the world's largest banks rushed in to rescue reckless shareholders. History has remained silent about the fate of the two million people who lost their jobs.

The free-trade revolution

That lesson went unheeded. In late 2008 the liquidation of several trillion dollars of derivatives by hedge funds, most of which were registered in offshore tax havens, worsened the financial crisis that had already begun in the United States, extending it to the entire world and touching off a recession that spared nobody. There are also, thankfully, many harmless global impacts of the new information technologies. But the example cited above returns us to the point made in the first chapter, namely that when things can happen instantly and universally, creating a new currency in a free country in a hostile political environment is impossible.

The other pillar of globalization is free trade, and the oldest of the many facets of free trade is the free circulation of goods. The second facet is the free circulation of services, which is already more complex since "services" can mean many different things, from banks to transportation, from education to culture, and more. Free trade of capital means that there are no obstacles to its circulation. Free trade of capital must be distinguished from the freedom to invest, under which anybody can invest without hindrance or controls anywhere, with no other obligation to the host country than respect of public order and decency. As we will see, this has had profound consequences on the development of the so-called emerging countries. Finally, the free circulation of manpower enables individuals to work where they wish, providing that they have the skills required in the country of their choice.

These facets of free trade did not come into existence at the same time in the form of valid and achievable objectives. Only recently have we begun to realize that all were necessary if we were to speak of a truly globalized world—the result of a lengthy evolution that requires some background explanation to understand what is happening today.

Revisiting the ruins

One of the many impacts of the Great Depression of the 1930s was a radical increase in trade barriers in the form of customs duties and quotas. Countries strived to protect their own industries at the expense of those in other countries. Each country hoped to export its own unemployment to its neighbours. The targeted country would in turn impose its own tariffs, and gradually trade barriers sprang up everywhere. Exports, sales, and employment then plummeted everywhere. Fear that escalation of this kind could happen again has haunted countries ever since. Trade barriers based on tariffs and quotas were reinforced during World War II with the addition of exchange controls. Essentially, the countries at war were in need of foreign currency reserves to be able to import the required raw materials for the war effort and to import the arms that were not produced domestically.

When the war ended in 1945, Europe had spent all its gold and foreign currency reserves (i.e., United States dollars), yet a major reconstruction and arms industry conversion effort was required.

Only the United States enjoyed an abundance of basic goods, which Europe was unable to purchase without drastically reducing imports to the bare essentials. Two years after the war, Europe experienced disastrous harvests combined with an extremely harsh winter. The vicious circle was spiraling out of control. The United States was producing the required grain crops and coal, but Europe hung on the edge of bankruptcy. Two far-reaching measures were adopted. The first was the Marshall Plan, named after the Chief of Staff of the United States armed forces who went on to become President Truman's Secretary of State. The United States government offered substantial amounts of aid to European countries to finance reconstruction, but on condition that the receiving country provide an equal amount of credit to its European partners. Trade was thus able to resume gradually. It was simple and straightforward but amazingly effective. The USSR forbade the Central and Eastern European countries it occupied from taking part. Europe was thus divided in two and the iron curtain came down, only to be lifted forty years later.

The second initiative was even more substantial. In that same year (1947), twenty-three countries, primarily Western European and North American, signed a trade agreement that became known as the General Agreement on Tariffs and Trade (GATT), referred to in Chapter 1. The agreement was intended to reduce— and possibly eliminate—the customs duties and quotas that had stifled international trade. In the beginning it only covered goods, and by no means all goods. Clearly, it would take light years to dismantle the barriers of agricultural protectionism. Member countries then began what came to be known as "rounds" of negotiations on the basis of one constraint and one instrument. The constraint was that each member could reduce trade barriers but could not increase them. The instrument was simple—and proved to be very effective: it was the most-favoured nation clause or MFN and was applied as follows. Let us say that Germany considered Canada a good market for its paper machine. But since Canada's customs duties were too high,

German machines were not competitive. Germany would then propose that Canada reduce duties by thirty percent and in return would agree to roll back duties on the mining machinery that Canada had been trying to sell to Germany for years. If Germany and Canada reached an agreement, the most-favoured nation clause would mean that the duties agreed upon by Germany and Canada would automatically apply for all GATT member countries.

The most-favoured nation clause became a powerful lever to gradually reduce customs duties from one round of negotiations to another. Each round proved to be laborious, probably owing to the initial formula that resembled duty barter. The negotiating process was eventually streamlined, but the fundamental principle of the most-favoured nation clause remained the same. Among members of the "club," trade grew smoother and less expensive, while those who were not members saw the gap widen between the customs duties imposed on their goods and those applied to goods produced by "club" members. Unsurprisingly, everybody wanted to join and take part. Equally unsurprising is the fact that existing members imposed conditions for new members wishing to join! China had to wait for years to be accepted. Russia is still not a member. Today more than 150 countries are members, not of the GATT, but of its descendant, the World Trade Organization established in 1995. The changes in 1995 went far beyond a simple name change.

Organizing the world

The World Trade Organization lies at the heart of globalization. It is where rules are set and where failures, setbacks and achievements are registered. The WTO reflects our ability to manage world affairs, far more than the United Nations.

The WTO is based on the fundamental principle of non-discrimination, which is the objective of each and every member country. Countries join, each with its own battery of protective measures. Each country is expected, from one round to another, to reduce these measures until they eventually disappear. Two instruments are used to ensure non-discrimination, the most-favoured nation clause, of course, and the national treatment clause, which provides that a foreign company will be treated in the same manner as a national company. Negotiating methods with one hundred and fifty members at the table obviously differ from when there were only twenty-three. Consensus is the rule. In other words, a measure or set of measures will not be enforced unless a consensus is reached. This clause is particularly important because it protects small member countries from the huge trading powerhouses. A small country is on much firmer ground than if it had to negotiate alone with major powers.

The World Trade Organization can also impose sanctions. Should it be established that a member country is violating the rules of the organization and that other member countries are suffering losses, the latter can apply proportional countervailing measures by way of compensation.

To summarize, an international trade legal system has gradually developed, one that can ensure compliance. There is, however, little or no room for idealism. If all member countries except Costa Rica and Guatemala agree on a measure, for example, the measure will be adopted. But if all members except for the United States or the European Union agree, the measure will not be adopted.

Defending small countries

By the same token, a country can win its case on losses suffered because of another country's policies, sometimes without even using the countervailing rights recognized by the World Trade Organization. For example, although Canada won every one of its cases against the United States in the softwood lumber dispute, it did not dare use countervailing measures, choosing instead to negotiate to obtain the best result.

The protection provided small countries by the World Trade Organization is striking nonetheless. The story of the Cotton Four crisis in Africa is an excellent example. Cotton is a vital crop in West Africa. Mali, Burkina Faso, Benin, and Chad produce high quality cotton but have difficulty selling it. Spain, Greece and above all the United States subsidize their cotton growers substantially. In November 2001, when the Doha Round of trade negotiations began, the African countries concerned filed a report on United States cotton subsidies prepared for them by Oxfam. That report revealed that the American government distributed four billion dollars in subsidies to the country's twenty-five thousand cotton producers, a practice that clearly corrupts competition, discriminates against African cotton, and violates the rules of the World Trade Organization. Many African countries are among the world's poorest, often depending on international aid, and as such are in no position to negotiate. They demanded that the United States reduce and even eliminate subsidies to cotton producers. The United States refused and the chief American negotiator even suggested that the Africans abandon cotton and turn to other crops. The African cotton-producing countries then approached the so-called BRIC countries (i.e., Brazil, Russia, India, and China) for support. Faced with American intransigence, those countries decided to scupper the round of negotiations for a while. Within the World Trade Organization, no small country need stand alone.

This is a key point. For so long Quebecers have been told that as an independent country they would be weakened and driven to their knees. Hence the necessity of pointing to the rules that now govern international trade.

The basic principle underlying the World Trade Organization, namely non-discrimination, tends nonetheless to limit the use by developing countries of policies that favour economic growth. Furthermore, in times of recession, most countries, regardless of their level of development, are pressured by public opinion to curtail trade liberalization. Finally—and most important—in certain economic sectors the principle of non-discrimination makes absolutely no sense.

Out of WTO reach

Every state that wishes to have its own cultural policy automatically runs afoul of World Trade Organization rules governing cultural goods and services. Providing funding to artists, for instance, will inevitably be seen as discriminatory. Such support is provided for national artists, troupes, groups, and organizations and not to foreigners. The national treatment rule makes no sense.

A country cannot even dream of having its own national cultural policy without resorting to explicit protectionism, which might take the form of quotas for national music on the radio or films produced domestically on television or in movie theatres, and financial incentives, such as tax credits and book publishing grants.

It was unreasonable to expect that the World Trade Organization would establish rules applicable to trade in cultural goods and services that went against policies incompatible with its principles. The alternative was to address UNESCO. The idea of a Cultural Diversity Charter was first proposed in the Francophone Summit Organization and it then rapidly won support among Latin American and Latin countries in Europe. Gaining German support marked a turning point. The United States, which had withdrawn from UNESCO in 1984, decided to rejoin that organization when they realized that their cultural interests were being challenged. That country's films, videos, and music are among its largest exports. The United States government was still attempting to limit the scope of certain provisions, and still had not ratified the agreement when this book went to press. Whatever the eventual outcome, it is clear that the World Trade Organization's "jurisdiction" over culture is virtually a dead letter.

Quebec finds itself in a paradoxical situation. Together with France, Quebec led the fight for an agreement on cultural diversity and therefore for the responsibility of the state to protect language. In Canada, however, that means that the federal government, and not the government of Quebec, is responsible under the new agreement to protect and promote the French language in Canada. It came as no surprise that the federal government jumped at the idea. As a consolation prize, Ottawa promised Quebec a seat at UNESCO, but later admitted, along with everybody else, that it was not really a seat since Quebec is only a province.

Recognition that culture could be kept beyond the reach of the World Trade Organization was a powerful precedent. Though imperfect and somewhat shaky, it remains nonetheless unparalleled. A distinction was gradually being drawn between goods and services that are traded commercially, and thus covered by the World Trade Organization, and others that by nature are not commercial goods or services. That does not mean that they are not governed by international rules, but they cannot be dealt with under regular commercial trade rules.

Education is a case in point. Universities are regularly spinning off campuses throughout the world. Most are American, but certain European countries have begun to follow suit. Many countries are obviously ready to welcome them and even provide financial support. Others tolerate them, but refuse funding. It is clear once again that the principle of non-discrimination and the national treatment clause cannot be invoked to force host countries to apply the same funding system to these universities that is used to support "native" universities. On another but similar level, recognition of degrees earned through Internet is already raising problems that current provisions cannot resolve.

Health-care services present a very specific problem. Multi-national corporations now provide home care and are opening clinics. Will they be treated in the same way as the multinationals that provide goods and services in other sectors? Should the national treatment clause be applied to these health-care multinationals? The main issue in the health-care sector, however, is that of patents. The World Trade Organization set January 1, 2005 as the date when all member countries had to recognize the patents registered in other member country territories. Most patents are registered in a small number of member countries. By extending what amounted to monopoly power, the World Trade Organization effectively condemned research in countries that were just beginning to develop the sector. In the case of prescription drugs, poor countries were placed in an untenable situation at a time when certain emerging countries, Brazil and India in particular, were able to supply generic medications at low cost. Without going into the details, suffice it to say that the pharmaceutical multinationals backed away from imposing their patents on a certain number of drugs used to fight AIDS, malaria, and tuberculosis in Third World countries. Once again it became clear that there were limits to how broadly World Trade Organization rules could be applied.

Water will raise serious problems. Is it a marketable commodity? It is quite obviously marketed in some places. Equally obvious is the fact that companies that control water in any given place will sell it at monopoly prices. It is also true that riots for water against the Bechtel Corporation in Bolivia left some people dead. Should the World Trade Organization, however, be trusted with responsibility for establishing rules for access to water?

Consider the North American example of James Bay. For many years, the idea of building a dyke across James Bay to separate it from Hudson Bay has been mooted. The water flowing from Quebec and Ontario rivers into James Bay would gradually transform it into an inland fresh water sea. A canal would then bring that water to Lake Superior where it would be used to supply the American Mid-West beset with chronic water shortages and sinking water tables.

The scenario is anything but science fiction. A chapter of a book by former Quebec Premier Robert Bourassa describes the scheme in detail.[1] The scheme, known as the Grand Canal, was promoted by Tom Kierans more than fifty years ago; Kierans had also managed to interest many leading federal politicians in the scheme. But if water is a marketable commodity subjected to the rules of the World Trade Organization and, by the same token, to NAFTA, Quebec would be prohibited from maintaining an embargo on exports of water in bulk.

To summarize, more and more decisions affecting our daily lives are made at the international level and this tendency will intensify. During recessions like the one that began in late 2008, protectionism is a very real risk. Furthermore, we are not likely to see any major free-trade offensives launched during such periods.

It should also be noted that we still lack a clear idea of the limits to the application of free trade. At what point is the capacity of a country to influence the rate and orientation of its growth called into question? The saga of the Multilateral Agreement on Investment in 1998 provides interesting lessons.

Early in this chapter, we saw how control of exchange rates after World War II hampered and could even stop international trade. Free trade was generally restored in Western countries by the end of the 1950s. The Soviet block remained closed until the 1990s. That period is now considered to be history, and nobody misses it. Capital now circulates freely.

Business versus government

The notion gradually spread that if capital can circulate freely, then the investment of capital should be equally free. Extending the notion of capital to investment is abusive. The freedom to move capital is that and only that. It means that money, in whatever form, can travel freely from one country to another: a fundamental feature of globalization. Freedom to invest is another matter entirely. It means that a foreign company can

---

1. Robert Bourassa, *Power from the North*, Montreal, Prentice Hall of Canada, 1985, 181 p.

move into a country and assume none of the obligations imposed by the government of that country other than respect for public order and decency. The chief executive officer of the Swiss-Swedish company ABB, an international heavy electrical equipment manufacturer described in very clear terms what globalization meant for the firm he heads. "I would define globalization as the freedom for my group of companies to invest where it wants when it wants, to produce what it wants, to buy and sell where it wants, and accept the fewest possible restrictions coming from labor laws and social conventions."[2]

The ABB chief executive officer was describing what would be the ideal situation for multinationals like his, with facilities in dozens of countries and whose subsidiaries negotiate among themselves to the point that similar arrangements account for almost half of international trade. A country that could potentially host such investments will obviously think twice before rejecting the influence of foreign businesses wishing to establish facilities within its jurisdiction as development could well depend on those investments. In any case, it requires a healthy dose of confidence in the good faith of the "invisible hand" to take on the challenge.

One attempt was made. In 1997, without informing the public, countries in the Organization for Economic Cooperation and Development or OECD (i.e., the world's most industrialized economies) began negotiations on a Multilateral Agreement on Investment that seemed to be inspired by the above declaration. It was taken for granted that if developed countries could agree among themselves, that agreement could easily be imposed on developing countries or, more specifically, those countries that had the most to lose and that were the least capable of resisting the North America-Europe alliance. For an agreement like that to work, the governments concerned would have to agree on an

---

2. Quoted in Jacques Parizeau, *L'AMI menace-t-il la souveraineté des États?* (Does the MAI Threaten National Sovereignty?) L'action nationale, January 1999, pp. 38-54.

arbitration body to rule on the issues arising during treaty implementation. Governments sometimes lack imagination in comparison with multinational corporations, but they still can legislate. The conspirators—by no means an exaggeration since the treaty was negotiated behind closed doors—agreed to establish an international arbitration tribunal whose decisions would be binding on governments. What's more, only corporations—not governments—could appeal to the proposed tribunal.

That was going too far. When the draft treaty showed up on the web, it shocked anyone who had not sworn allegiance to neoconservative fundamentalism, but above all it woke up political leaders whose delegates, it seemed, had only briefed them partially and badly. A few days before the final round of negotiations began, the prime minister of France declared to the French National Assembly basically that although countries might wish to delegate certain aspects of national sovereignty to international bodies, it was not acceptable to hand them over to private interests. He ordered the French delegation to withdraw from negotiations and the entire structure came tumbling down.

The demise of the Multilateral Agreement on Investment is noteworthy because it shows that globalization is hardly a Sunday afternoon picnic. Nation-states maintain their ability to resist. But nothing is ever absolutely settled. The draft agreement on the Free Trade Area of the Americas (FTAA) included foreign investment provisions inspired by the Business Council of the Americas (the official advisor to negotiations) and analogous to those of the Multilateral Agreement on Investment. Brazil effectively derailed negotiations on the FTAA. The government of Canada nonetheless still attempts to include similar provisions in all bilateral trade agreements negotiated with developing countries.

Quebec and the next bid for sovereignty

If complete liberalization of investment had been agreed upon under the Multilateral Agreement on Investment or the Free

Trade Area of the Americas, the Quebec model—sometimes known as Québec Inc.—would clearly have been illegal. Its combination of public and private interests provided obvious financial advantages to the latter in exchange for conditions that were incompatible with the spirit and the letter of the projected treaties. For example, the establishment of the Bell Helicopter facility in Mirabel just north of Montreal, which involved huge amounts of money (two hundred and forty million dollars) for technical manpower training, technology transfer commitments, and compulsory worldwide mandates, would have been in total violation of the draft Multilateral Agreement on Investment.

As a mere province of Canada, Quebec is generally unfamiliar with these issues. The Quebec government is kept at a distance from them and, due to their complexity, neither the media nor even universities can be expected to monitor them in any significant detail. In 2002 the Quebec government established a globalization watch agency (*Observatoire de la mondialisation*) to keep abreast of these developments. A year later the Liberal government abolished it for budgetary reasons.

When a federal government enters into a treaty it does not necessarily commit the federation's provinces or founding states when, even under the federal constitution, those provinces or states enjoy full and exclusive jurisdiction in certain defined areas, such as education, health or public procurement. However, as the scope of international negotiations widens, pressure is growing on federations to ensure that their signatures on treaties also commit their constituent parts. Each federation in turn has to find ways to encourage its provinces, states, or municipalities to accept the outcome, the usual solution being some sort of financial arrangement. Globalization is already a powerful centralizing force in federations, a tendency that can only grow stronger.[3]

---

3. It is remarkable the Canada protests to President Obama that the Buy American Act enables states and cities in the United States to bypass NAFTA commitments.

Description of the erratic but sustained expansion of globalization could go on and on. Environmental protection, for instance, has not been addressed even though it is *the* issue of the day, the only one that can mobilize millions of individuals who understand that they are at the heart of a major revolution and who demand that their governments act in what has become, of necessity, a global context (Kyoto). In Europe the roadmap has been drawn up and the issues are clear, but North Americans remain divided, confused, and at odds. Nothing is more surprising than to see certain American states adopt policies that are diametrically opposed to those of their central government. In Canada regional differences, which are addressed in Chapter 9, are acute and irreconcilable.

I have purposely avoided touching on establishment of free trade zones, customs unions or economic unions in this discussion of globalization. The previous chapter showed how the establishment of such large markets was essential in order for countries with small populations to prosper and develop, providing they paid close attention to the productivity of their companies and their ability to innovate. A country is no longer defined by its economy, but rather by its culture in the broad sense. It comes as no surprise to see that all peoples and all nations strive to define their own future, or in other words, to become sovereign. By the same token, when Quebec made a bid to become an independent country in 1995, it was marching in step with history. Establishment of large markets has opened the door to independence for the peoples and nations who desire it.

We go one step farther in this chapter. Globalization is expanding and intensifying and citizens have no way of opposing it. It would be as futile as attempting to stop the rising tide. But globalization can cause abuse, spiral out of control, and leave entire segments of society undefended. Citizens have only their government to turn to, the government they elected, and from which they can demand help and protection, just as it has been for centuries. In the beginning in fact, all they could hope to obtain from their prince or their republic was help and protection.

Even when countries form a well-integrated zone like the European Union, citizens continue to turn to their respective countries in times of crisis—and not only economic crises—threats or pandemics.

In fact, as globalization intensifies the sovereignty of nation-states grows even more essential. As governments delegate more and more of their powers to international organizations, citizens must be reassured that someone is looking after their well-being and protection. That someone must be the expression of a common culture and common institutions, most often with a common language, and above all of a desire to live together.

In this light the future of federations is seriously compromised. When a country is called on to commit itself on increasingly varied and numerous issues and to take part in ever more complicated discussions, it inevitably finds few advantages in a political structure that grants sovereign powers to its constituent jurisdictions on strategic issues like education, health, culture, and some types of financial institutions, or even commercial law. For domestic policy purposes, the central government already imposes its own priorities on its constituent jurisdictions by means of subsidies, shared programs, and fiscal incentives. In Chapter 9, we will see how the federal system in Canada, which was one of the most decentralized industrial countries, has gradually become centralized.

Quebec's next attempt to achieve sovereignty will be made under these conditions. In some ways nothing has really changed. Sovereignty or independence for Quebecers has always meant being responsible for their own future. That means having control of laws, taxes, and international treaties. As with other countries, Quebecers will delegate powers to international organizations. Nonetheless, though much is the same, a new perspective is slowly developing. Opening up to the world is not a wish, a desire or a virtue. It is in the order of things and has become inevitable. Becoming responsible for our own future can only be accomplished in the context of the entire world. To remain in Canada is to turn in on oneself. It means refusing to take part in defining our future.

Chapter 4

SOVEREIGNTY AND PUBLIC OPINION

The idea of independence has been maturing in Quebec for half a century. Two generations have debated the issue. Every year if not every few months, Quebecers are polled to determine how they would vote and how many support sovereignty, special status or Canadian federalism, outfitted with the appropriate adjectives: cooperative, centralized, asymmetric, and so on. These polls significantly influence the communication and electoral strategies of political parties and governments alike.

The half-century has been a windfall for semantics experts, as gaps in support widen or narrow depending on the words used in polls. The most favourable results, as we have seen, accompany the words "sovereignty-association." Then comes sovereignty combined with a proposed partnership, followed by unadulterated sovereignty, independence, and finally separation. The gaps vary over time but the order remains the same.

Fear and good government

Depending on the period, some view the promotion of sovereignty as dangerous from an electoral standpoint. It is therefore soft-pedaled as elections approach. Others claim that promoting sovereignty is key to mobilizing support. So goes the never-ending debate.

The fears, hesitation, and apprehensions associated with the objective of independence, which have been handed down from one generation to another, wax and wane from one election campaign to another. The widespread fear among the elderly, who were led to believe they would lose their federal old-age pensions simply because the federal government would disappear, now only makes us smile. On the other hand, the notion that preparing a referendum on sovereignty will prevent improving the health-care and education systems remains curiously tenacious. Referendum or health-care became the less-than-subtle slogan.

Quebec society, like all other developed countries, is faced with problems that transcend borders, such as how to prevent baby-boom generation indebtedness from becoming an unbearable burden on the next generations? Or what fiscal regime will foster development and growth without causing unacceptable social inequalities?

After the 1995 referendum loss, the Quebec government played down sovereignty and launched a crusade to balance the budget and attain a "zero deficit." What started out as a priority became dogma, and then practically took over public debate for years, opening the door to Ottawa, all but monopolizing public policy right up until the financial crisis and the accompanying recession radically modified the economic outlook starting in late 2007. The question must be asked: fifteen years after the 1995 referendum defeat, in the midst of a world-scale economic crisis, what does Quebec public opinion think of the objective of Quebec sovereignty?

The Bloc Québécois poll

The Bloc Québécois conducted a poll from March 11 through March 15, 2009 with 1,003 respondents (margin of error of ± 3.1%). The results were partially cross-referenced with polls conducted by CROP and Angus Reid at about the same time. The results do not always match the interpretations tossed about by certain pundits, and, when the results tend to converge, the data gain in credibility.

The Bloc poll did not measure respondents' voting intentions but evaluated their opinions. The first question is the one I have always wanted to ask; the simplest and clearest question that leaves no room for doubt: "Do you want Quebec to become an independent country?" For the entire sampling, the poll showed 49 percent in favour and 50 percent against. Among French-speakers, 56.3 percent were favourable and 42.9 percent opposed.

Never in the past has unadulterated independence received similar levels of support. The result was so surprising in fact that it makes one wonder if the poll was flawed. At approximately the same time, however, similarly phrased questions asked by CROP yielded results showing 49 percent support for Yes and 51 percent for No, after distribution of the undecided (as was done in the Bloc Québécois poll), while Angus Reid came up with 40 percent replying Yes and 41 percent No, before distribution of undecided respondents. Thus there was no flaw.

Since the major media conglomerates and the federal government also conduct polls, it was not surprising to see the media rise up in arms in May and June 2009 when the Parti Québécois brought the question of sovereignty directly to the fore once again. Though the answer to the Bloc's question may have seemed surprising, it was less so when different scenarios were suggested.

The first of these was: "Do you want Quebec to become a sovereign country in an economic association with Canada?" In all, 61.4 percent of respondents were in favour, and 36.9 percent opposed. Among French speakers, 66 percent were in favour, and only 32 percent were opposed.

Special status

The second scenario was: "Do you want Quebec to be part of Canada with a special status?" In all, 66.4 percent of respondents were in favour, including 67.3 percent of French speakers, which means those who spoke English or other languages responded very much like the French-speaking population. Special status was thus supported by all three segments of the Quebec population

From a constitutional standpoint, the question of special status was settled a long time ago. During a famous debate at a federal provincial conference between Prime Minister Pierre Elliott Trudeau and Quebec Premier Daniel Johnson senior, it became perfectly clear that the House of Commons could not possibly tolerate two categories of members, those who could vote on all legislation and those who represented Quebec ridings, who would either vote on legislation applying to all Canadians except Quebecers or would have to abstain from voting on certain laws that did not apply to Quebecers.

Special status for Quebec, from a legal and constitutional standpoint, is contrary to the equality of citizens before the law and the normal workings of a democracy. Settled in 1967, the question of a special status was never raised again. That did not prevent Quebec from establishing *de facto* its own particular system. Each time Quebec has been authorized to set up programs of its own distinct from federal programs, all the other provinces were also formally authorized to do the same thing but chose not to (e.g., the Régie des rentes du Québec, Quebec's pension plan, and the Caisse de depot et placement). A segment of a particular or distinct status thus came into being. We can confidently say that the special status that appears to muster strong support among Quebecers is either unthinkable and unrealizable (from a constitutional standpoint) or has been in force for a long time. In fact, many Quebecers have been known for years to be in favour of what comedian Yvon Deschamps has described as "An independent Quebec in a united Canada." For some it is paradoxical, for others, totally illogical. Not necessarily. When pressure for sovereignty grows too strong, committed federalists appear to prefer special status to a break-up. Committed sovereigntists who feel independence cannot be attained agree that special status is better than nothing at all. The problem, for both of these groups, is that establishing special status does not depend on Quebecers alone. It must be agreed upon by Canada in accordance with a constitutional amendment formula, which would be unthinkable or, rather, would only be thinkable if, after a winning referendum, Quebec were about to declare unilateral independence. But at that point, well...

The final scenario was: "Do you want Quebec to be part of Canada without special status?" For Quebec as a whole, 42.7 percent were in agreement and 54.9 percent, opposed. Among French speakers, support for that option dropped to 39 percent and opposition increased to 58.9 percent. These results were quite startling. At a time when politicians and media leaders considered generally that Quebecers are uninterested in constitutional issues, more than twenty-four percentage points—thirty among the French-speaking population—separated those who did not want special status for Quebec from those who did. And yet in a statement to *Le Devoir* on June 4, 2009, the leader of the Liberal Party of Canada, Michael Ignatieff, made it clear that the status quo is quite satisfactory for him. "It is out of the question to give more power to Quebec within the federation or to take any concrete action that would accrue to recognition of Quebec as a nation by the House of Commons."[1]

It's realistic, it can be done… but will it happen?

The poll also included a series of five questions designed to examine the responses with respect to Canada and the future of Quebec.

---

1. Hélène Buzetti and Alec Castonguay, "Pas question de donner plus de pouvoir au Québec," *Le Devoir*, Friday, June 5, 2009; ("il n'est pas question de donner davantage de pouvoir au Québec au sein de la fédération ou encore de faire des gestes concrets pour donner du relief à la reconnaissance de la nation québécoise par la Chambre des Communes."

1. It will be possible one day to reform Canadian federalism in a manner that will satisfy both Quebec and the rest of Canada.

	Overall	French-speakers
Agree	62%	61.7%
Disagree	34.6%	35.3%

2. Quebec has the right to separate from Canada.

	Overall	French-speakers
Agree	60.9%	68.2%
Disagree	37.5%	30.7%

3. Quebec has the human and natural resources and capital to become a sovereign country.

	Overall	French-speakers
Agree	59.9%	65.4%
Disagree	37.8%	32.7%

4. The sovereignty project can be achieved.

	Overall	French-speakers
Agree	56.6%	61.4%
Disagree	41.9%	36.9%

5. The sovereignty project will be achieved.

	Overall	French-speakers
Agree	34.4%	38%
Disagree	61.7%	57.5%

The 1995 referendum question was asked again, fourteen years later. That question referred to a bill tabled in the National Assembly and to the agreement signed by three political parties and may be difficult to understand today. But the results are surprising.

	Overall	French-speakers
Agree	49.7%	57%
Disagree	50.3%	43%

Overall, the result is almost identical to the 1995 referendum results, slightly down among those who speak French, yet slightly up among those who speak English and other languages.

To summarize, Quebecers are attached to a vision of a Canada that would agree to grant them a special place, a distinct status. Since that vision has never been fulfilled, a large number of them have turned to independence and the majority is now convinced that independence can be achieved... However, since they are by no means convinced that it will happen, they nurture the old dream of a federal system that, one day, will end up understanding what Quebecers want.

Looking back

Even if our understanding of the past helps us grasp its significance, the Bloc Québécois poll is, like any poll, nothing more than a snapshot taken at a given moment. But if we look more closely at some of the questions, it is possible to go back a few years. Below is a table as it appears in the poll.

Evolution of four estimators among the French-speaking population over time

	Reformed federalism (%)	Right to separate (%)	Resources for sovereignty (%)	Sovereignty is achievable (%)
April 1995	55	66	62	45
Oct. 1995	46	75	68	70
Oct. 2000	61	67	63	56
March 2009	62	68	65	61

The most striking observation is obviously the evolution of answers as to whether sovereignty is achievable or not. The leap that took place between April and October 1995 reflects several factors linked to the referendum campaign that intensified as the vote approached. Some fifty-five thousand people took part directly in regional commissions on Quebec's future, numbers never witnessed before or after. That rate of participation is even more noteworthy in that none of the mainstream television networks agreed to cover the meetings. Only the community television networks believed that it was in the public interest to broadcast the debate.[2]

During the same pre-referendum months, Quebec's restructuration ministry published a large number of studies that systematically analysed the budgetary, economic, administrative, and legal aspects of Quebec sovereignty. The political debate surrounding those studies and the inept manner in which they were presented undoubtedly limited their public impact, but those shortcomings do not appear to have cast any significant doubt on the impression that the government was ready to go ahead and knew where it was going.

Coordination between the three political parties (Parti Québécois, Bloc Québécois, Action démocratique du Québec) not only played a significant role at the grassroots, but also at the centre of operations, in defining strategy.

It would be no insult to the efforts made by sovereigntist leaders to assert that there is truth in the saying that "ideas lead the world." In April 1995 a mere forty-five percent of Quebecers believed sovereignty to be attainable, whereas a mere six months later seventy percent of the same people believed it to be attainable, despite fierce debates and fear mongering. In October 2000, five years later, the Parti Québécois still held power in Quebec City. Its priorities had changed, its support for sovereignty had gone from active to passive, but its fight against the deficit was very active. The zero deficit goal led to so many budgetary cutbacks that the federal government, which, because of the reduction of transfer payments, had made that a goal far more difficult to achieve, then rushed to the rescue of Quebecers who had no alternative.

---

2. In contrast, the public hearings of the Bouchard-Taylor Commission on reasonable accommodations that were religiously covered by Radio-Canada, and were considered to be a success, only managed to obtain the participation of five thousand people.

Voter wisdom

In all this confusion, people reacted with their proverbial wisdom. They were less convinced that sovereignty could be achieved: support dropped from seventy percent to fifty-six percent. That figure was nonetheless much higher than at the beginning of 1995, and it continued to rise gradually, reaching sixty-one percent in 2009. Efforts to discuss, persuade, and convince have not been entirely in vain.

Many more people hope and believe however that federalism can be reformed. In October 1995, only forty-six percent of the population believed it possible. Since the Quebec government itself must rely on the federal government to help maintain the basic programs that its own austerity measures were jeopardizing, people understood. If the Quebec government acts as though federal reform, or at least federal indulgence, is the only solution, voters will follow suit: the proportion of the French-speaking population who believed that Canadian federalism could be reformed reached sixty-one percent in October 2000 and remained virtually the same (sixty percent) nine years later.

In March 2009, in short, sixty-one percent of French speakers think that sovereignty is achievable while sixty-two percent think that federalism can be reformed. Only thirty-eight percent think that sovereignty can be achieved.

It's all as clear as mud. At first glance, French-speaking Quebecers don't seem to know which way they want to go: they can choose between two equally tempting options. With the first possibility, namely remaining part of Canada but with special status, a vast number of insurmountable hurdles pop up each time Quebec tries to improve its constitutional status or formally enhance its powers. From an administrative standpoint, although significant advances were made years ago, they have turned out today to be illusions (the "seat" at UNESCO is undoubtedly the most striking example).

The second option, independence combined with special links with Canada, is not credible for a majority of Quebecers, even though it is desirable for the largest number. The drop in credibility can be explained by factors that include frustration over a debate that has been going on too long, lack of confidence in Quebec leaders over many years, and weaknesses of a public discourse that has not adapted to change.

The main danger in the current situation is that the status quo, which satisfies nobody but which everybody ends up tolerating, becomes acceptable by default. That is basically what has happened with the 1982 Constitution, which every political party in Quebec has rejected ever since its adoption. Quebec's collective rejection of that Constitution has had no practical impact, and has in no way hindered the day-to-day business of the federal government nor resulted in any legal consequences or proceedings before the courts. In fact, Quebec has looked on while the only status that it explicitly rejects—namely that of being a province like all the others—has been confirmed.

The only way to avoid this outcome is to bolster the credibility of the sovereignty option, and that can only be accomplished by making it more relevant, and by bringing out its advantages, both domestically and in the face of globalization.

Age distinctions in voting patterns change

The final point to this chapter deals with the evolution in support for sovereignty by age group and the evolution of the age groups themselves. These data are important in establishing an accurate diagnosis of the impact of demographics on changing attitudes. Between 1995 and 2009, support for the Yes in a referendum varied significantly from one age group to another. Among 18 to 24 year olds, support for the Yes fell from 61 to 55 percent. Among 25 to 34 year olds, the drop was negligible and within the margin of error. However in the 35 to 44 year old group, namely those who were between 20 and 30 in 1995, the drop is significant, falling from 59 percent to 47 percent.

Among older people, the situation is inversed. Among 45 to 54 year olds, the increase was negligible, within the margin of error. Among the 55 to 64 year olds, the increase is significant, jumping from 42 percent to 54 percent. In the over 65 group, a moderate increase is observed, going from 35 percent to 38 percent.

In short, a shift is underway that also changes the perspective, as the age pyramid reinforces the observed changes.

Number of electors by age group — 2009 compared to 1995

18-24 yrs − 11,000	45-54 yrs +393,000
25-34 yrs − 287,000	55-64 yrs +292,000
35-44 yrs − 25,000	+ 65 yrs +291,000

These data can be interpreted in two ways. One would be to conclude that the idea of an independent Quebec was that of a generation, basically the baby-boom generation, and that young people today are more interested in individual success than in a collective project. The other is to observe that the age group in which support of the Yes option dropped the most—the 35 to 44 year olds who were very involved and active in the 1995 referendum—emerged from their twenties, disappointed at the loss in 1995, and faced with political debate and activity dominated by, or should we say obsessed with, problems of accounting and management. That group of young people had a rude awakening. Today's young people have taken up political action again, and with increased support for sovereignty among older segments of the population, who have the numbers on their side, sovereignty could be achieved, that is, on the condition that political strategies are based on a realistic vision of the changes that have occurred.

Chapter 5

CONSTITUTIONAL ILLUSIONS

I have wasted a lot of my time on and around the Canadian Constitution. Supreme Court rulings demand close scrutiny since in a country governed by the rule of law they must be complied with. There can be no doubt, however, that the federal government always wins, either legally or financially. Duplessis put it quite accurately when he said, "The Supreme Court is like the Tower of Pisa. It always leans in the same direction." Supreme Court judges themselves are not necessarily partial, but the Constitution is simply made that way. The federal government can tax in all areas and its spending power is unlimited. It can legislate in the name of "peace, order and good government." Moreover, it can disavow all provincial legislation even though it no longer uses that power. It is no longer necessary. The provinces got the point a long time ago. Section 92 of the Canadian Constitution recognizes that the provinces have sovereign powers in specific areas such as education. However, for years, the federal government assumed half the expenses of technical or post-secondary schools. It has recently turned its attention to research, but without taking into consideration what the provinces might want. It then created university "research chairs," which contractually must always be labelled "Canada Research Chairs," as well as scholarships and bursaries. In practice, Ottawa does what it wants... or, at least, most of the time. The Quebec question keeps things somewhat tense.

Without Quebec, Canada would have no more constitutional problems than the United States has. Financial transfers would settle most issues. We do not fully appreciate how the United States has settled major social problems, such as bussing to integrate schools, simply through financial arrangements. Since transfers are conditional on the adoption of federal norms, what Washington wants, it gets.

Which government is the real one?

In 1964 Jean Lesage pulled Quebec out of twenty-nine cost-sharing programs in which the federal government covered half the costs and decided on how the money was to be used. Many of those programs were in areas of provincial jurisdiction (i.e., education, health-care). Quebec obtained a fiscal rebate of 16.5 percent of the basic federal income tax rate in addition to a financial transfer. All the other provinces could have followed suit, but none did. The following year, Quebec created its own pension plan, the Régie des rentes, set up a mechanism for financing the plan and created its own investment agency, La Caisse de dépôt et placement. The other provinces were free to do the same, but none did. In 1967, the federal government established a deposit insurance system. Quebec and Ontario then each created one too, but Ontario joined the federal system only one month after launching its own. Twenty years later Quebec took over responsibility for occupational training. All the other provinces could have done the same, but only Quebec wished to do so. Ten years later it was the same story with parental leave programs, with the same results.

In short, for two generations Quebec has gone it alone while the other provinces are perfectly happy with federal government responsibility for these new programs. Sparks fly occasionally. For instance, Quebec is not alone in opposing the federal government's move to establish a single Canadian securities commission. Similarly, no grounds for agreement on natural resource management have been found, nor on greenhouse gas reduction commitments. Without Quebec, however, agreement could easily be reached, despite serious regional differences. In Canada, as elsewhere, such differences do exist. But that is not the question. For Canadians the federal government is a real government. The Charter of Rights has become the symbol of a real country. That was not always the case. For a long time people in rural Saskatchewan could not understand why their cousins in North Dakota earned more for their wheat and paid less for their cars. To the east many Newfoundlanders felt for many years that they had made a mistake when they joined Canada. That has all been settled now. When a Canadian is dissatisfied with the Liberal government, he or she will vote Conservative or NDP. When a Quebecer is dissatisfied with a Canadian political party (a federalist party), he or she will be drawn towards sovereignty. That is why the Quebec national question will simply not go away. English Canadians and new Canadians know which country they live in and have no identity problems when they sew the Canadian flag on their backpacks, which is simply a way of saying who they are. The young Quebecers who similarly put the *fleur de lys* on theirs are not as certain of who they are. For some the gesture has a cultural significance, for others, it is a political statement. Sorting things out can be tricky. These youngsters deserve some respect, considering the lack of determination that some sovereigntist leaders have displayed.

The "beautiful risk"

The best example of this cultural tug-of-war is the dramatic attempt by Canadian federalists to win the hearts and minds of Quebec sovereigntists. In some ways, this part of Canadian history resembles a Greek tragedy. Before describing it, I would like to underscore the good will with which the operation was launched. Though the good will did not last forever, and political infighting ended up pushing it aside, it is important to understand that it all began with a very real, frank and honest effort to provide Quebec with a significant place in Canada and to "put the country together again": what René Lévesque called the "beautiful risk."

Patriation of the Canadian Constitution in 1982 left sovereigntists, and particularly René Lévesque, deeply scarred. One need only think back to the "night of long knives" during which the provincial premiers, who had up to that moment supported René Lévesque's position, abandoned him and reached an agreement during the night with the federal government—they even went to the trouble of waking up the premier of Manitoba in Winnipeg where he had returned to campaign in provincial elections. René Lévesque, who spent the night in a Quebec hotel on the other side of the Ottawa River, woke up to find that the agreement had been reached behind his back and that the Constitution would be patriated with modifications that took powers away from the National Assembly that it had held before the Parliament of Canada had even been created. Quebec had lost the 1980 referendum two years earlier but the Parti Québécois had been returned in 1981. In addition, a brutal recession had set in. With pressure mounting from all sides, the Quebec government moved rapidly on the economic front (Corvée-Habitation and an accelerated investment program were striking examples of this). But what was to be done on the constitutional front? How was Quebec to resume the struggle with Ottawa?

Brian Mulroney, who had taken over the leadership of the Conservative Party, was elected in September 1984 after making an important speech in Sept-Îles in which he proposed to bring Quebec back into Canada "with honour and enthusiasm." On November 19, 1984, René Lévesque answered Mr. Mulroney's call and agreed to take the "beautiful risk." Sovereignty would remain the "ultimate insurance policy" but, for the time being, Quebec would play loyally in the federalist arena. However that arena would have to adapt to a substantial Quebec presence.

The Quebec cabinet imploded. Seven ministers and elected members resigned. Shortly thereafter, René Lévesque resigned too. My goal in recalling those events is not that of a historian. For twenty-three years, I worked for and with René Lévesque and still have the greatest admiration and esteem for him. Though we were never close friends, the cause we shared and towards which we had worked so hard and so effectively, led us to respect one another. I had agreed to work under him. When the breaking point came I had to leave and he had to do his duty. At the end of that wonderful adventure, which ended so sadly, there was no reason for either of us to feel any shame about what had occurred. The remarkable team built by René Lévesque fell apart, certainly not with enthusiasm, but surely with honour.

Meech

In 1985 the Parti Québécois was defeated and the Liberal Party under Robert Bourassa came to power. Brian Mulroney was still convinced that Quebec had to be brought back into the Canadian constitutional framework. With the Liberals in power in Quebec, it was seen to be a much easier task. Moreover, Robert Bourassa, who was still burdened by the failure of the 1971 Constitutional Conference in Victoria during his first term in power, replied to Prime Minister Mulroney's invitation with five conditions under which Quebec would agree to be part of the Canadian Constitution. He declared: "Never has Quebec demanded so little from the rest of Canada nor applied more minimal conditions." One condition dealt with Quebec's specificity: the Canadian Constitution would recognize Quebec as a distinct society. For Quebec, that was a minimum, and not just a question of common sense. In 1985 the Quebec National Assembly had recognized eleven Aboriginal peoples as "distinct nations."

In Canada it was another story. Little by little a handful of ideas were transformed into values that defined the Canadian nation. The most important of these, as mentioned above, was the Charter of Rights. In a country where colour and race have mingled since the end of the nineteenth century but where the

WASPs (White Anglo-Saxon Protestant) held sway, the Charter created a deep and lasting impression, and the rigour with which the courts applied it had rapidly enhanced its credibility. The second idea, which would appear to contradict the first, was multiculturalism. Obviously, and particularly in the West, the Ukrainians, the Poles and the Chinese, not to mention the Aboriginal peoples, greatly outnumbered the French-speaking population. The idea that Canada had two founding peoples no longer appeared to make any sense. In Toronto, the idea seemed little short of ridiculous. Yet to avoid a break-up, it was impossible for Canada to be anything but an officially bilingual country. With varying degrees of difficulty, official bilingualism was introduced, mainly in federal agencies, but also in New Brunswick and in regions of Ontario close to Quebec (including Ottawa) at the same time as the founding idea of multiculturalism. The operation was not easy. A considerable number of English Canadians believed that their children would be better Canadians if, through French immersion courses and exchanges with Quebec, they came to accept the rules of bilingualism and a real individual biculturalism. Others experienced official bilingualism as a constraint imposed by history and an unnecessary complication to life.

Everybody found common ground however in the Charter of Rights. At least under the Charter all citizens were equal, regardless of origin, roots or particular characteristics. And then along came those Quebecers who upset the applecart as usual by asking to be recognized as different and distinct, first as a society, but—who knows?—perhaps as individuals at some later date. During the debate on the Meech Lake Agreement, more and more English-speaking Canadians spoke out against it. The fact that the provincial premiers had agreed unanimously carried little weight. The premier of Newfoundland, who had already expressed doubts, gradually became the ordained defender of the "real Canadians." In Quebec, Premier Bourassa, who had considered his constitutional demands to be an absolute minimum, was faced with an Opposition Leader who implored him not to abandon anything from the "most minimal demands Quebec had ever formulated," but which were now transforming him into a radical in the eyes of English Canada.[1]

In desperation, the first ministers called on some high profile jurists to draft a legal opinion confirming that the Meech Lake Agreement had no constitutional impact and, in short, meant nothing from a legal standpoint. "While nothing in that clause [distinct society] creates new legislative authority for Parliament or any of the provincial legislatures, or derogates from any of their legislative authority, it may be considered in determining whether a particular law fits within the legislative authority of Parliament or any of the legislatures."[2]

It was all to no avail. The Manitoba Legislature refused to ratify the Accord, and it was not even presented to the Newfoundland House of Assembly. We would do well to remember what Meech was intended to achieve in order to grasp the magnitude and extent of the failure. The complete text of the agreement signed on June 3, 1987 begins: "WHEREAS first ministers, assembled in Ottawa, have arrived at a unanimous accord on constitutional amendments that would bring about the full and active participation of Quebec in Canada's constitutional evolution..."

The Bélanger-Campeau Commission

What was to be done after the failure of Meech? People had gotten the message. Quebecers would be either Canadians like everybody else, or they would have to go it alone. But Quebecers were not completely alone since free trade negotiations with the United States had ended at about the same time.

---

1. Readers might recall that I was Leader of the Official Opposition at that time.

2. Letter to Prime Minister Mulroney signed by six jurists (Messrs Beaudoin, Cameron, Edwards, Hogg, Swinton, Tassé), June 9, 1990.

Support for sovereignty soared. Ottawa stepped up constitutional debate by organizing seminars and consultations but it soon became apparent that the Quebec question was developing into a Canadian crisis. In Quebec City, a strange phenomenon could be noticed. The federalist premier and the sovereigntist leader of the opposition developed a working agreement, rather as they had done to make free trade with the United States a bipartisan issue. From the constitutional standpoint, Premier Bourassa had stated to the National Assembly the evening after Meech failed: "Quebec is, today and always, a distinct society, free and capable of assuming its destiny and its development." As Leader of the Official Opposition, I replied: "And I say... to *my* Prime Minister: I reach out to shake your hand. Let us try to find our bearings. We must find another route."[3] Together we decided to create a commission to study Quebec's future. The commission members would represent all political tendencies and would be appointed jointly by both party leaders. Premier Bourassa appointed Michel Bélanger, Chief Executive Officer of the National Bank, as one co-chairman, as leader of the Opposition, I appointed Jean Campeau, Chief Executive Officer of the Caisse de dépôt et placement. All political parties represented in Quebec City and Ottawa were represented, as were broad sectors of civil society. The public hearings sparked intense interest, but it quickly became apparent that support for sovereignty and for remaining part of Canada remained virtually identical. Some dramatic efforts were made, most of them in good faith, to compromise on a number of thorny issues. The commission ended up recommending that two parliamentary committees be created, one to examine any proposals that Canada might make to Quebec and the other to study the consequences of sovereignty. In addition, it was decided that a referendum would

3. Robert Bourassa: "Le Québec est, aujourd'hui et pour toujours, une société distincte, libre et capable d'assumer son destin et son développement." Jacques Parizeau: "Et je dis... à *mon* premier ministre: je vous tends la main. Essayons de nous retrouver. Il faut que nous puissions trouver une autre voie." Débats de l'Assemblée nationale, June 22, 1990, pp. 4134-4135.

be held between June 8 and June 22, 1992 or between October 12 and October 26, 1992. This referendum was to be on Quebec sovereignty. The proposals were adopted by a majority of commission members, with both the Liberals and the Parti Québécois members of the Quebec National Assembly voting in favour. It was nonetheless agreed that signatories to the commission report could include comments. It was also apparent that the usual political divisions had not dissolved, and so the bill tabled based on the Bélanger-Campeau recommendations included a preamble that clearly indicated that the government had no intention of achieving everything that was in the bill.[4] Nonetheless, in order to pressure the government to keep its commitment to hold a referendum on sovereignty by October 12, 1992, the Parti Québécois launched a petition that was signed by a million Quebecers. In the United States, proportionally speaking, that would be the equivalent of forty million signatures well before the availability of Internet polling. Each and every name was written by hand.

Charlottetown

A referendum was held in 1992. Not on the Bélanger-Campeau Commission recommendations, but on the Charlottetown Agreement.

While tremendous amounts of time and energy were being expended in determining the future status of Quebec, the Mulroney government had understood that the demise of Meech stemmed from polarization on the Quebec question. If progress were to be made in bringing Quebec into Canada, it could not be accomplished by making more concessions—or what appeared to be concessions—to Quebec. Canada in its entirety needed to be thought through once again. In short, ten years after the patriation of the Constitution, people set out to reevaluate the

---

4. An act respecting the process for determining the political and constitutional future of Quebec (1991).

entire foundation laid down by the fathers of confederation. The new "fathers" of confederation, in addition to the prime minister, would include all the first ministers of provinces and territories and four representatives of the Aboriginal nations. The agreement would be ratified in a referendum and not by each of the legislatures, as had been the case with Meech. Premier Bourassa managed to ensure that the referendum in Quebec would be conducted under Quebec's Referendum Act. Aboriginal nations organized their own specific referendum. Three distinct electoral colleges were established.

The text of the Charlottetown Agreement, as adopted by first ministers and Aboriginal leaders, comprised twenty-one pages. It was quite obviously drafted with the best of intentions, but it left many questions to be negotiated sometime down the line. Others were little more than vague or ambiguous proposals. In a nutshell, the agreement was reached quite smoothly since no serious attempt was made to deal with specifics.

The aspiring new fathers of confederation were probably aware that their new text was less than perfect, which explains why they were in no hurry it to make it public. In Quebec, those opposed to the agreement published an annotated edition using comic strip bubbles. Volunteers distributed two million copies to all households in Quebec.

On referendum day, 56.7 percent of Quebecers rejected the Charlottetown Accord, while 54.8 percent of English Canadians also rejected it. A strong majority of Aboriginal voters also rejected it. Whereas the leaders of the three electoral colleges had unanimously supported the accord, their respective populations opposed it. The leaders did not resign their positions and behaved as though nothing had happened. In some ways, they did the right thing. A four-year psychodrama had produced nothing in spite of the favourable context and conditions. These included a government in Ottawa that was so well disposed toward Quebec that it had induced the Parti Québécois to accept a "national affirmation" position, and the federalist government in Quebec that was so politically adroit that it had people believing it would be the one to bring about Quebec sovereignty, while at the same time it was very determined to bring Quebec into the Canadian Constitution. Such a winning combination would be hard to duplicate. Yet, when the dust fell, nothing had changed. By then, many people had given up looking for constitutional arrangements as a possible solution. It was time for the sovereigntists to take the initiative. Their time had come.

I will not rehash the 1995 referendum campaign, which I dealt with in detail in Chapter 2. The important thing is to understand the sequence of events. From whatever standpoint, from failure of the Charlottetown Agreement in 1992 to the 1995 referendum loss, the status quo, which was buttressed by the failure of both initiatives, came to be seen as the only possible outcome. However, Quebec and Ottawa reacted in completely different ways.

Zero deficit

With the change in government in Quebec that followed the 1995 referendum came a change in strategy. The new government was sovereigntist, but after the traumatic 1995 defeat, it acted as though the referendum had been a bad dream. When rumours began circulating about voting irregularities, the government did nothing, refusing even to investigate. Only when groups of political activists decided to look closer was any action taken, such as in Sherbrooke where courts found out-of-province students at Bishop's University guilty of voting illegally. Gradually it became clear that at least fifty-four thousand people had voted even though they did not have Quebec health insurance cards, which meant that they were not Quebec residents and thus did not have the right to vote. Quebec's chief electoral officer, the Directeur général des élections, investigated and confirmed these figures.[5]

---

5. Robin Philpot, *Le référendum volé*, Les éditions les intouchables, 2005, pp. 95-96.

These were the years during which the Quebec government devoted its time and energy to eliminating Quebec's budgetary deficit. When the Parti Québécois came to power in 1994, the anticipated deficit stood at six billion dollars. In fact for fiscal year 1994-1995, ending on March 31, 1995, the deficit was 5.8 billion dollars. During the referendum year, the media claimed that in order to win the referendum the government would have to "buy" the public sector unions whose collective agreements were expiring, and thus simply throw money out the window. The fact is that when the books were closed on March 31, 1996, the deficit had been reduced to 3.9 billion dollars. The Quebec government then decided to achieve a zero deficit just when the federal government was drastically cutting transfer payments to the provinces to balance its own budget. Quebec then undertook to achieve a zero deficit by adopting a strict fiscal agenda and reducing spending. Easier said than done. To achieve its objective the government would have to cover all its current expenditures and investments without borrowing, an unfeasible commitment. There is no shame in borrowing to pay for investments, either for a government or for an individual. Highway construction expenditures were also directly added to the debt, and only depreciation was included as a budgetary expenditure. Moreover, since the government had promised not to increase taxes, it made school boards increase school taxes, which made it possible for the government to reduce planned education expenditures.

In the race to achieve accounting purity in 1997, a major reform in accounting practice increased public debt with one fell swoop by twenty-five percent (from eighty to one hundred billion dollars), touching off a collective panic that lasted several years. The panic was fueled each year by an increase in debt, even though the deficit was zero. Investments were being directly attributed to the debt as only depreciation was considered to be a budgetary expenditure.[6]

---

6. The exact figures are seventy-eight and ninety-eight billion. Plan budgétaire, ministère des Finances, 2009-2010, p. J-16.

But the Quebec government was now living in fear. The search for money drove the government, and money was always welcomed wherever it came from. Practically speaking, it would come from Ottawa, which was only normal since Quebecers pay taxes to Ottawa and thus have the right to get some back. Ottawa was not about to play hard to get. A veritable storm of research chairs swept through Quebec universities. The lucky research chair holders, however, had to fully identify their benefactor. The prime minister of Canada was seen, for instance, summoning his Quebec counterpart for a photo-op while inaugurating the widening of the highway between Chicoutimi and Quebec City. Quebec ministries, hamstrung by treasury board guidelines, found the resources they needed from federal government sources. In short, the Quebec state was quietly becoming the province of Quebec once again.

Some might observe that financial and economic questions take up too much of this discussion of constitutional questions, yet that in fact is what was so tragic. A sovereigntist government that had almost achieved its goal of creating a country then plunged into financial austerity, obediently lining up behind "generally accepted accounting principles" and, in desperation, became indebted to the federal government. The mystery behind that rapid transformation remains to be clarified.

Sponsorship scandals

Unlike Quebec, Ottawa was sitting pretty. It could boast a balanced budget and was, in fact, swimming in surpluses generated by keeping contributions to unemployment insurance (now employment insurance) at high levels. The federal government was in an ideal position to return to the political and constitutional arena.

The referendum had frightened Ottawa. Every effort had to be made to avoid a repeat. Two major operations were undertaken, one aimed at winning the battle for public opinion—the

sponsorship scandal—and the second at sealing off the constitutional question—the Clarity Act.

The sponsorship operation began shortly before the referendum and lasted for several years. The idea was quite straightforward. The federal government would sponsor all sorts of
sports, cultural and community events so as to depict itself as a
true and powerful friend. Enormous amounts of money were
made available to a single senior civil servant who, during the
Gomery Inquiry hearings, well before going to jail, eloquently
described the atmosphere in Ottawa at a time when Quebec was
striving to balance its accounts by convincing hundreds of
doctors and thousands of nurses to take early retirement. "It was
war," declared Charles Guité.

At the same time, the federal government adopted the so-called
Clarity Act. To understand the concerns that preceded the Clarity
Act, it is necessary to return to the bill on Quebec's future that, as
head of the Quebec Government, I had had distributed to all
households in Quebec. That document stated clearly and explicitly
that if negotiations following a majority Yes vote failed in the year
following the referendum the Quebec National Assembly could
declare Quebec independence. That is the source of the idea that
Quebec could declare independence unilaterally. When I published
my book, *Pour un Québec souverain*[7] in 1997, a Quebec reporter
believed that he had found proof in the book that in the days following a Yes vote, I would in fact have declared Quebec
independence. This raised quite a flap. The Quebec National
Assembly, of which I was no longer a member, went into one of its
occasional mood swings—as it did with the "Michaud Affair" in
2001—and after everybody had denied any knowledge of the plan,
I found myself at the head of a conspiracy (of one person with
himself) aimed at declaring the unilateral independence of Quebec.

It was quite obvious nonetheless that in Quebec, following
such a tight race in 1995, those who were upset at the idea that a

---

7. Jacques Parizeau, *Pour un Québec souverain, op. cit.*

fraction of one percent of the voters might make them lose their country as they knew it, were not about to abandon their goal if one day we might win, even by a small margin.

The Supreme Court and clarity

The federal government then referred the question to the Supreme Court in the hope of obtaining an opinion that basically would make it illegal to declare unilateral independence. The Supreme Court was trapped. As indicated earlier, the 1967 Constitution does not prohibit a province from seceding. Even more curious is the fact that, after the 1980 referendum, the Constitution was amended following patriation in 1982 but no mention was made of a province separating. The argument can be made that when a province pulls out, that move effectively amends the Constitution, but it is a weak argument. In short, the federal government asked the Supreme Court to use its legal authority to settle a political problem.

The Court emerged relatively unscathed from the operation. Everybody got a piece of what they wanted.[8] The definition of unilateral secession is perfect. "Rather, what is claimed by a right to secede 'unilaterally' is the right to effectuate secession without prior negotiations with the other provinces and the federal government."

To my knowledge, nobody who has been elected in Quebec has ever made such a demand; the definition therefore raises no problems. Negotiations have always been part of the plan. The judges reciprocated by saying that if the sovereigntists who wish to negotiate were to win a referendum, the rest of Canada would be under the moral obligation to agree to negotiate. We sovereigntists were delighted to hear that. But the question and the result had to be clear. That made the federalists happy.

---

8. See my open letter to Supreme Court judges, "Lettre ouverte aux juges de la Cour suprême," in *Le Devoir*, September 3 and 4, 1998.

Unfortunately, however, the judges defined neither what a clear question consisted of nor what percentage would be considered to be a clear result.

The judges had no choice but to consider the possibility that if negotiations were ever initiated, they might fail. What would happen then? Though they did not reply directly to that question, they wrote:

> Although there is no right, under the Constitution or at international law, to unilateral secession, that is secession without negotiation on the basis just discussed, this does not rule out the possibility of an unconstitutional declaration of secession leading to a *de facto* secession. The ultimate success of such a secession would be dependent on recognition by the international community, which is likely to consider the legality and legitimacy of secession having regard to, amongst other facts, the conduct of Quebec and Canada, in determining whether to grant or withhold recognition.[9]

The observation by the Supreme Court judges went to the heart of the matter. It explains the efforts expended since the early 1990s to obtain, through recognition by France, a movement that would bring the United States to follow suit. It will remain true both generally and specifically for any new attempt by Quebec to become a sovereign country. As before, sovereignty's opponents can be counted upon to try and derail that process. That, more than anything else, is what explains why the federalists are hovering about so close to French President Nicolas Sarkozy. Fortunately, the future lasts a long time. We will be returning to the subject later.

The so-called Clarity Act was drafted based on the Supreme Court opinion. If the federal government believed that the referendum question was not clear enough or the result not clear enough, it would refuse to negotiate with a Quebec government that had won a referendum on sovereignty. Since the Supreme Court opinion did not clarify what clarity meant, the federal

---

9. Ibid., Section 155.

government, in its infinite wisdom, would dictate the definition and thus the law.[10]

The Quebec government reacted by asserting the rights of the Quebec government and public debate raged. Interestingly, I think, Cardinal Jean-Claude Turcotte, Archbishop of Montreal, summed it up best: "It is up to the people to decide and not the Supreme Court."[11]

From a political standpoint, the impact of that episode on public opinion cannot be underestimated. Drawing on a Supreme Court opinion, the federal government now claimed to be in a position to block Quebec independence even after a majority yes vote. For that reason, whatever strategy is adopted by a sovereigntist government, it must never be forgotten that the best way to convince Canada to negotiate in good will is for Canada to be made to understand that if it does not wish to negotiate, Quebec can go ahead on its own (i.e., keeping the Canadian dollar, through free trade with the United States, and so forth). Moreover, it is hard to imagine Canada refusing certain agreements, such as free circulation between Ontario and the Atlantic Provinces or use of the St. Lawrence Seaway.

To sum up, once the people have spoken, more than a few problems will solve themselves, and though the naysayers may rant and rave, there will be little they can do about it.

---

10. Clarity Act, An Act to give effect to the requirement for clarity as set out in the opinion of the Supreme Court of Canada in the Quebec Secession Reference, assented to on June 29, 2000. Quebec's response was the Act respecting the exercise of the fundamental rights and prerogatives of the Quebec people and the Quebec State (Bill 99), adopted on December 7, 2000.

11. *Le Devoir*, December 29, 1997.

Chapter 6

THE INTERNATIONAL OUTLOOK

Some may be surprised to see a discussion of the international outlook so early in a section dealing with Quebec's next bid for independence. It is nonetheless consistent with my approach thus far, based on the principle that Canada will do everything it can to prevent Quebec independence because without Quebec its national identity with respect to the United States will quickly become a problem—and its role in the world will be diminished. I have always believed that Quebec's success would be conditional on obtaining popular support within Quebec and significant recognition internationally. Both are necessary in order for Canada to reconcile itself with the idea of an independent Quebec. Moreover, once it becomes clear that our capacity to negotiate is based on our ability to do without negotiations, then I believe we can look forward optimistically to arriving at a civil and acceptable outcome.

The Supreme Court opinion on Quebec secession referred to above has a permanent validity that is not weakened or altered by the so-called Clarity Act. Should negotiations fail, the decisive factor following a Quebec declaration of independence would be recognition by the international community. That acceptation— it cannot be described as a recommendation—would be critical. It answers the question: What would happen if negotiations fail? And it points out that the answer will come from the international community.

In Quebec, people are not properly prepared to recognize the importance of international initiatives in settling the national question. These initiatives are perceived to be somewhat exotic. Some people consider them to be posturing. That is why I want to underscore how essential international initiatives are to win recognition of Quebec as an independent country as rapidly as possible after a referendum victory and after the Quebec National Assembly, using the powers conferred upon it, declares Quebec independence.

Preparations take a long time and are complicated by a previous failure. When I set out to re-launch the sovereignty movement in 1988, our international credibility was virtually nonexistent. Between then and January 1995, when many influential people came out in our support during my official visit to Paris, many initiatives were undertaken, culminating in a proposal from President Mitterrand to appoint a person to establish a direct link between the two of us, without intermediaries.

In the United States, our many meetings with senators and governors did little to bring us closer to the White House, with the exception of a single contact with a representative of the National Security Agency that proved to be very useful.

Contacts were also made with French-speaking African countries, often torn between their long-standing and sometimes active support for Quebec and the unlimited funds being doled out by the federal government.

Today, after the 1995 referendum and after the many years during which the idea of Quebec independence was gradually put on a back burner and public opinion perceived it to be less urgent, the international relations that had been established by Quebec sovereigntists also gradually broke down. The Liberal government that took over in 2003 chose nonetheless to remain active on the international scene. It brought pressure to bear on the Canadian government to open free-trade negotiations with the European Union and signed an agreement with France governing mutual recognition of professional and skilled manpower.

But the federalist Liberal Party could hardly be expected to give the slightest political tinge to its international relations. Relations with the United States have been reduced to trade and economic issues. The Canadian government, for strictly electoral reasons, promised to grant Quebec a seat at UNESCO. But once the election was over, it was clear that the seat was little more than a folding stool that could only be opened with Ottawa's approval.

Messrs Sarkozy and Desmarais

The Sarkozy incident took place in late 2008 and early 2009. It was a curious event that has completely upset Quebec's relationship with France in the short term. In fact his statement was ridiculous, scandalous even, and is little more than a caricature of how money moves politics. Money usually abhors publicity. But in this case, politics proved itself thankful to the point of parody, for money past and money future.

The main actor in this spoof was Nicolas Sarkozy, an ambitious young politician who early on joined Jacques Chirac's entourage. After being a right-wing prime minister under the Socialist President François Mitterrand, Chirac ran unsuccessfully against Mitterrand in 1988. After his defeat, he withdrew to the Paris mayor's office to lick his wounds. President Mitterrand appointed Chirac's closest ally, Édouard Balladur, as prime minister, but it was understood that Chirac would run for president in the 1995 French elections. Liking power, however, Balladur abandoned Chirac and prepared to run for president with the support another Chirac man who thought he smelled power. That man was Nicolas Sarkozy. Jacques Chirac won the election, Balladur withdrew, and Sarkozy was lost in limbo.

He was soon brought back to life by billionaire Paul Desmarais, who had parlayed a prodigious sense of what to buy and sell and when to do so into a fortune. Desmarais is less an entrepreneur than a financier. He is also fascinated by politics. A convinced federalist, he has fought all is life against the sovereigntist movement. His career really took off in Quebec, though he was born and raised in Sudbury, Ontario. It was not long, however, before he sold off all his Quebec holdings except for his newspapers (he owns seven of the Quebec's ten French-language dailies) and his huge estate known as Sagard located in the Charlevoix region between Quebec City and Chicoutimi.[1]

Though Desmarais has maintained substantial interests in English Canada, particularly in finance and insurance, he has become, together with his long-time Belgian associate Albert Frère, one of the most powerful businessmen in France and Belgium. A leading or major shareholder of GDF-Suez, Total, Lafarge, and other less well-known companies, his business sense is equalled only by has ability to sniff out political talent in Canada, in Quebec, and in France.

Within months after taking power, Nicolas Sarkozy awarded Paul Desmarais the *Grand-croix de la Légion d'honneur*, the highest distinction given by France, an astonishing award for a businessman. Reading President Nicolas Sarkozy's glowing account of the services rendered by Paul Desmarais, not to France, but to Sarkozy himself, is particularly entertaining. But the flights of mutual admiration between the businessman and the French politician have completely destabilized the triangular relationship between Quebec, France, and Canada. The Quebec-France relationship was already showing signs of stress. Months after his election, so intent was President Sarkozy on pleasing his powerful friend that Quebec's very federalist premier, Jean Charest, had to tone things down and for all intents and purposes disavow the hyperactive French president. And Paul Desmarais, after granting a seven-page interview to the French weekly *Le Point*, quietly withdrew to the role he likes best: pulling strings without making waves.

---

1. See Robin Philpot, *Derrière l'État Desmarais: Power*, Les Intouchables, 2009, 208 p.

If quotes could kill...

The following quotes give a clear indication of how Quebec was dropped—not by France, but by France's Head of State.

"Quebec today is far from being a priority for France. One only need to observe the disappearance four years ago of the annual alternate trips to one another's country made by the prime minister of France and the premier of Quebec." (Christian Rioux, correspondent for *Le Devoir*, July 6, 2007).

"Over time Nicolas Sarkozy became a close friend of the Desmarais family and a regular visitor to the Sagard estate. 'In fact,' he said yesterday evening, 'if I am President of the Republic today, I owe it in part to the advice, friendship and loyalty of Paul Desmarais.'" (Lous-Bernard Robitaille, correspondent for *La Presse*, February 12, 2008).

"Jean-Pierre Raffarin [former prime minister of France] informed us that President Nicolas Sarkozy would use his visit to Quebec City next October to jettison France's Quebec policy, a policy based mainly on the principles of 'Non-interference and non-indifference.'" (Louise Beaudoin, *Le Devoir*, April 1, 2008).

"To begin with, the 'new French position' on normalization represents a clear rejection of shared France-Quebec action over the past forty years. The Government of France had long been a major, and even essential, partner in ensuring the existence and development of Quebec's diplomatic network." (Jean-Marie Girier *et al.*, *Le Devoir*, April 4, 2008).

"'You know that we are very close to Quebec, but I wish to say that we also like Canada very much as well. Our friendships and loyalties are not pitted against each other. We bring them together so that [...] the future of Canada and France will be the future of the two countries,'... declared Nicolas Sarkozy, who was speaking without notes." (Robert Dutrisac, *Le Devoir*, May 9, 2008).

"His [Jean Charest's] low-key, four-day trip to Bordeaux, Brouage and Paris was in no way comparable to the festivities inaugurated by the Governor General Michaëlle Jean ten days earlier at La

Rochelle that drew 10,000 people. Jean Charest had to make do with a brief ceremony..." (Christian Rioux, correspondent for *Le Devoir*, May 20, 2008)

"He [Nicolas Sarkozy] declared: 'I am one of those Frenchmen who consider Quebecers to be our brothers and Canadians to be our friends.'" (Christian Rioux, correspondent for *Le Devoir*, May 23, 2008)

"At the heart of the great Canadian people, there is the Quebec nation. [...] For your message is a great one, and a useful one, for it brings together the ardent defence of identity, language and culture, but also the refusal to turn inwards upon oneself. The Quebec people are not sectarians." (Nicolas Sarkozy before Quebec's National Assembly, October 17, 2008)

"This time, Stephen Harper did not wait twenty-four hours to change his tune and admit that the pompous high-flying declarations by Sarkozy about re-founding capitalism were of no interest to him." (Christian Rioux, correspondent for *Le Devoir*, October 24, 2008)

"'Frankly, if anyone here would like to say that today's world needs an additional division, then we do not have the same reading of the world,' he [Sarkozy] declared a few hours before the Francophone Summit opened in Quebec's capital city." (Jocelyn Royer, correspondent for *Le Droit*, October 18, 2008)

"In one of the published answers to written questions submitted by *La Presse*, Mr. Sarkozy made it clear that in his mind 'the era of referendums on Quebec sovereignty is over.'" (Michel David, *Le Devoir*, October 18, 2008)

"The historic leader of the independence movement, former Premier Jacques Parizeau, pointedly observed that when he made known his preference, President Sarkozy, the most powerful elected leader in the French-speaking world, went much further in rejecting Quebec independence than had President Clinton, the most powerful leader of the English-speaking world. During the 1995 referendum campaign, Mr. Clinton had complimented Canada, but keeping his options open and resisting pressure from Ottawa, refrained from denouncing the independence movement and asserted that the decision belonged to Quebecers, which Mr. Sarkozy avoided saying."

(Jean-François Lisée, *Le Devoir*, October 25, 2008, reproduced from *Le Monde*, October 24, 2008)

"'Let's be honest: the policy of non-interference and non-indifference that has been the rule for years, is just not my thing,' he [Sarkozy] declared at the Palais de l'Élysée. 'Quebec is my family, Canada, my friends,' he added. The French Head of State said he rejected 'division,' 'sectarianism,' 'turning inwarsd' and 'hatred'." (Tommy Chouinard, *La Presse*, February 3, 2009)

"Refusing to judge Nicolas Sarkozy's statements, Premier Jean Charest chose his words carefully. In his opinion, the policy of 'non-interference and non-indifference' has not been discarded. Jean Charest even stated that 'if ever there is another referendum,' he could see 'no other possible policy for France.'" (Christian Rioux, correspondent for *Le Devoir*, February 3, 2009)

"It is well known that the President of France abhors upstarts. Since Quebec seems not to understand that Canada is the President's new flame, he decided to express himself in his own inimitable way, 'Casse-toi, pauvre con!' (F*** off, you idiot). The most striking thing was not his diatribe against Quebec sovereigntists, but the discomfort it caused Premier Charest who will have ambivalent memories of the day he was decorated the Legion of Honour." (Michel David, *Le Devoir*, February 5, 2009)

"The statements also sparked a reply from the leaders of the Parti Québécois and the Bloc Québécois who, in a letter, declared that no foreign head of state had ever shown such disrespect for more than two million Quebecers who voted in favour of sovereignty in the last referendum. Referring to the letter signed by Pauline Marois and Gilles Duceppe, Mr. Sarkozy claimed that, since his election, he had begun to rebuild the France-Quebec relationship by providing it with new momentum and expanding areas of cooperation." (Alexandre Robillard, *Le Droit*, February 14, 2009)

Powerful offstage interests

It was mind-boggling! Of Quebec's two hundred elected members in the Quebec and Canadian parliaments, one hundred and one are registered members of parties that support the goal of Quebec independence. The French president's insults, his scornful dismissal of a broad cross-section of the Quebec people—and a strong majority of the French-speaking population—most probably cost France some very old friends. All to please his favourite billionaire? To a certain extent perhaps, but not exclusively. There had to be other reasons, probably business-related. Sarkozy's anti-Quebec broadside coincided with his term as president of the European Union, which made him a key player in the G-20 meeting that he saw as an opportunity "re-found" capitalism. He needed support from Canada as a G8 member; slapping Quebec in the face was a surefire way to get it.

Nuclear energy was also a long-term factor. Nuclear energy is used to produce seventy-eight percent of France's electricity. Government-owned AREVA is the flagship of France's nuclear development program. In Canada, Ontario would soon have to refurbish its aging nuclear generating stations, operated on the struggling Canadian CANDU technology. In Western Canada, extracting oil from tar sands requires enormous amounts of energy, possibly using nuclear power.

AREVA is clearly a contender and already controls uranium deposits in Canada. Should the government of Canada decide to sell off Atomic Energy of Canada, AREVA would be a possible buyer. With the help of GDF-Suez and Total, of which Paul Desmarais is a leading shareholder, AREVA would surely be on the short list for the construction of nuclear generating stations in Ontario and the West.

Any decision on these questions would be made by the governments of Canada, Ontario, Saskatchewan, and Alberta.

If Paris was "well worth a mass" for Protestant King Henry IV, and if opening the door to the Chinese market is well worth promising not to raise the issue of Tibetan independence, then, by the same token, the possibility of obtaining contracts valued in the tens of billions of dollars is well worth strong words of support for Canadian unity.

But the strategy might just not work. Prior to the 1995 referendum, I was warned that the Canadian Navy was on the market for four submarines and that France might let Quebec drop for a while in order to bid on the contract. The threat was staring us in the face. A new French foreign minister by the name of Alain Juppé refused to "drop" Quebec. His loyalty will not soon be forgotten.[2]

Still, Mr. Sarkozy's statements completely changed the international perspective, at least in the short term. One unintended consequence was that they revealed the depth of support Quebec enjoys in France. The French media paid little attention to the story, but the people that former Prime Minister Raymond Barre called the "microcosm" were scandalized. Nothing however is more important for heads of state or heads of government than saving face; we can hardly expect the current president of France to lose his.

France is still there...

Should we rule out a role for France in Quebec's bid for independence for a few years? The answer is no, but our approach will have to change. The links between Quebec and France are much closer and more diversified than we realize. For many years now they have grown and developed in a number of ways. Every year some two thousand young Quebecers and another two thousand young people from France cross the Atlantic thanks to the *Office franco-québécois pour la jeunesse*. Quebec welcomes from three to four hundred thousand French tourists each year (except for a slight drop early in the 2000s). Quebec businesses have been operating in France for a long time now, and exchanges and internships have grown steadily. In the arts, Quebec singers and creators have been immensely popular in the French-

---

2. As could be expected, the British consortium won the contract.

speaking world for a very long time now. [3] French-speaking Africa has been a constant preoccupation of the federal government and its financial arm, the Canadian International Development Agency (CIDA) since the 1970s. But most of the agency's personnel are from Quebec. While the Quebec government has been virtually absent, except in the immigrant selection process, the number of African students studying in Quebec universities continues to grow.

Everything that can be done should be done to enhance future relations with the French people on the one hand and with French-speaking Africans on the other. It should also be a priority for Quebec to open a Delegation in one of the countries of the Maghreb, for instance, and another in a leading African country south of the Sahara.

In the same vein, the agreement with France on mutual recognition of professional skills is an outstanding achievement—the type of initiative that will bring the two people closer together over the long term. The initiative was taken by Quebec Premier Jean Charest who, after being decorated by Mr. Sarkozy and having listened to the torrent of abuse heaped upon his fellow citizens, quietly explained that if there were another referendum, he did not see how France could adopt any other position than that of non-interference and non-indifference. Nothing could be clearer, but time will be required.

Relations with American states

Political relations with the United States are quite straightforward. In the run up to the 1995 referendum, the government of the United States maintained official relations with Quebec at a level commensurate with that of any other Canadian province. Successive ambassadors in Ottawa declared that the

---

3. The remarkable work of the France-Québec associations also deserves mention.

United States considered Canada to be a partner and a friend and that the Quebec question concerned the Canadians, while one went as far as to use the words "Canadians and Quebecers." James Blanchard, who was ambassador in 1995, suggested, as a threat, that an independent Quebec could not automatically expect to participate in the North American Free Trade Agreement. As we noted earlier, despite the pressure brought to bear on President Clinton in the days before the referendum he did not veer away from his position in favour of Canadian unity while adding that the question should be decided democratically.[4] Since then, as could be expected, the Quebec national question has vanished from radar screens in the United States.

This does not mean that Quebec's specificity has not been demonstrated, particularly on environmental issues. Quebec public opinion was awakened early by the Kyoto Treaty. Protecting the environment has been a long-term concern for Quebecers; debate has rarely been a partisan affairs. In a striking display of solidarity, fifteen thousand Quebecers demonstrated against construction of a gas-fired generating station. Far from being a symptom of the NIMBY syndrome, the turnout was a show of pride in what had been accomplished through the use of our own clean hydropower.

But the American and Canadian political environment has generally not been well suited to this type of concern. For years, the United States government, until the election of President Obama, refused to endorse the Kyoto Treaty and even to recognize human impact on climate change. In Quebec, even an aggressive opponent of sovereignty like former federal Liberal Party Leader Stéphane Dion contrived to win admiration because of his energetic defence of environmental policies. It turned out to be a flash in the pan. The formation of a minority Conservative government in Ottawa showed how acute was the conflict

---

4. See Chapter 2, p. 58. For détails on pressure exerted on President Clinton, see Robin Philpot, *Le référendum volé, op. cit.* pp. 139-147.

between Western Canada, which wished to protect the spectacular expansion of its oil industry, and those who in Canada, and particularly Quebec, refused to abandon their commitment to environmental policies.

Particular attention should be paid to Quebec's relations with the Maritime Provinces and Ontario, and with some American states whose policies differ from those of their federal government. California of course comes to mind. That state, even though it has had its constitutional knuckles rapped on occasion, has contributed more than any other to modifying American energy policy.

From a Quebec standpoint, however, the most interesting case is that of the Green Paper published in 2006 on climate change, which is the subject of an entire section of the final chapter of this book. That Green Paper referred directly to an agreement reached in 2001 by the provinces of Eastern Canada and the New England States and which, in certain of its provisions, was borrowed directly from California. Such direct bilateral contacts will multiply. The trend is already visible in such sectors as trucking and softwood lumber production.

From a strictly political viewpoint, contacts between Quebec and neighbouring states should be maintained and encouraged. We generally understand the importance of such contacts when they concern electricity, but we sometimes underestimate the extent to which our neighbours can be of assistance in modifying or softening decisions made by the American federal government.

Beyond the United States, France, and the French-speaking world, relations with other countries should not be neglected, even though they cannot be as systematic and often result from specific circumstances or personal contacts. For instance, for two years running I attended the International Social Forum in Porto Alegre, Brazil. It was astonishing to observe the depth and the number of contacts that Quebec trade union and non-governmental organizations had with officials close to President Lula and with some of his cabinet ministers.

In totally different circumstances, the Ambassador of Sweden came to see me before the 1995 referendum in Quebec City at a time when rumours had it that some French authorities were considering abandoning Quebec. "France was the first country to recognize the United States after the war of independence," he told me. "Sweden was the second. If we can be of any help to you..." There was surely some irony in that unfinished sentence, but one never knows. The Ambassador of the Netherlands at the time was very much opposed to Quebec sovereignty and made his position known in no uncertain terms. These things must be monitored closely.

Humanitarian aid

Finally, it appeared to me that, among the international relations a new country must develop with the rest of the world, the highest priority must be assigned to humanitarian aid. Such a policy would present few problems for Quebec as hundreds or thousands of Quebecers have been and are involved in humanitarian projects worldwide. Not only does the Quebec government know virtually nothing about what its citizens do overseas, it doesn't even care to find out. As soon as I was elected Premier in 1994, I established a humanitarian aid service that Dr. Réjean Thomas agreed to head. We began with Haiti for obvious reasons. What Dr. Thomas with his small budget managed to accomplish with schools and dispensaries in rural areas was amazing. His position was eliminated as soon as I left government. The Quebec government continues to allow the federal government, the Desjardins movement or Oxfam-Quebec take on responsibilities that should be its responsibility. Soon after leaving the Quebec humanitarian aid service, Dr. Thomas founded Médecins du Monde.

Chapter 7

IS AN INDEPENDENT QUEBEC VIABLE?

When the question is asked, the answer sounds like a balance sheet. Does Quebec receive more money from Ottawa than it contributes? Quebec's contributions consist of the different kinds of taxes paid by citizens and companies to the federal government. Ottawa in turn provides Quebec with pensions and allocations to Quebec citizens, contracts and subsidies to Quebec companies, and payments to the Quebec government (e.g., equalization payments).

Quebec's share of the federal government's assets and debt must also be established. Quebecers have a right to a share of assets held by Ottawa, but they also have to assume responsibility for a share of the federal debt that was contracted on their behalf. When Quebec becomes independent, Quebecers must pay interest on their part of the net federal debt, or the debt minus assets.

This is a somewhat simplified version of an accounting exercise that has been done regularly, if my memory is right, since 1965. If it purports to show that Ottawa spends much more in Quebec than Quebec sends to Ottawa, the federalists cry victory, as they— and the media—did during the 1980 referendum. If the same exercise proves the opposite, then the sovereigntists cry victory, but since they have less influence on the media, their victory cry is not heard quite as loudly—as when Parti Québécois finance critic François Legault published his in-depth study in 2005.

These are no more and no less than accountants' figures, snapshots of the situation at a given time. Depending on the time chosen, snapshots can show very different pictures. Still, these calculations are essential to understanding what is happening and what may happen. When for generations people have constantly hammered away at the idea that there are "have" and "have-not" provinces, that the "have-not" provinces receive equalization payments while the "have" provinces do not, and that Quebec alone receives almost sixty percent of all equalization payments made to the "have-not" provinces (that means billions of dollars), those same people are well placed to convince others that independence is a pipe dream. It takes columns of figures, a bit of pedagogy, and a lot of patience to overcome these fear-inducing caricatures.

The first part of this chapter is based on a study conducted by François Legault, the former Parti Québécois Member of the National Assembly for the riding of Rousseau and Finance and Economic Development Critic for the Official Opposition. The text is entitled *Finances d'un Québec souverain* (Finance in an Independent Quebec).[1] Before looking at François Legault's figures, let us briefly review earlier studies that have, over time, made it possible to establish a method for calculating and presenting the situation.

Accounting studies: Bélanger-Campeau

The first study of this kind made public was conducted and released in 1973 in time for the Quebec general election. For the first time, the Official Opposition had presented a draft budget that was nothing less than a budget for an independent country. It was entitled "Budget for Year One," namely 1975-76. As author of that budget it is difficult, thirty-five years later for me to assess the validity of the exercise. One thing is certain: its presentation

---

1. The study was published in a brochure form.

during a televised debate did not go down in history as a stunning success. It was obviously easier to explain the concept of income elasticity of taxation in a university classroom than in front of a television camera.

After the demise of the Meech Lake Accord, the Bélanger-Campeau Commission on the political and constitutional future of Quebec was set up. The Commission Secretariat, headed by Henri-Paul Rousseau, future CEO of the Caisse de dépôt et placement, conducted several studies including one entitled *Analyse pro forma des finances publiques dans l'hypothèse de la souveraineté du Québec* (Pro forma Analysis of Public Finance in the Case of Quebec Sovereignty). It set out the state of public finances that could be expected to prevail in a sovereign Quebec for the year 1990-1991. It sought to determine how much it would cost the Quebec government to provide the same federal services, but without evaluating overlap costs.

"Following its deliberations, the Bélanger-Commission concluded that '[...] the repercussions on public finance of Quebec's acceding to sovereignty would be minimal whatever the expenditure scenario might be.'"[2]

In Chapter 5, we noted that after the Bélanger-Commission tabled its report, the Quebec government under Premier Robert Bourassa set up two commissions made up of parliamentarians, one with a mandate to study constitutional proposals that could be developed by the federal government and the other to study the consequences and impacts of Quebec sovereignty. The latter commission called for briefs from those who wished to submit them, but instead of taking a position and choosing an option, it simply collected the conclusions of all the reports received. Is an independent Quebec viable? All of the possible answers were listed, ranging from a resounding Yes, through a variety of equivocal Yes's, to unequivocal No's.

---

2. Bélanger-Campeau Commission Secretariat, *Analyse* pro forma *des finances publiques dans l'hypothèse de la souveraineté du Québec*, p. 492, quoted in *Finances d'un Québec souverain*, p. 11.

The Restructuration ministry's accounting studies

In 1994, in the new Parti Québécois government, I created a ministry for Restructuration mandated to study the modifications that would be required in Quebec public administration if, after a referendum victory, Quebec were to become independent. Among the many studies conducted with the help of the Institut national de la recherche scientifique (INRS), as well as many Quebec civil servants and external consultants, three focussed specifically on questions of public finance: *L'état des finances publiques d'un Québec souverain, Le partage des actifs et des passifs du gouvernement du Canada* and l'*Étude sur la restructuration administrative d'un Québec souverain*:[3]

The first study, conducted by actuary Claude Lamonde and Pierre Renaud of the Institut national de recherche—Urbanisation, sought to establish the income and expenditures of a sovereign Quebec for the year 1993-1994. It used the Bélanger-Campeau Commission methodology and was posited as a neutral exercise in which no rationalization or budgetary choices were made. The authors of the study concluded that "a sovereign Quebec would be viable from the standpoint of public finance."

The second study *Le Partage des Actifs et des Passifs du gouvernment du Canada* conducted by actuaries Claude Lamonde and Jacques Bolduc used a different method than the one established by the Bélanger-Campeau Commission—the authors concluded that since assets and the debt had not been incurred during the same period they had to be dealt with separately. It also concluded that a sovereign Quebec was viable from the standpoint of public finance.

The third study, entitled *Étude sur la Restructuration administrative d'un Québec souverain* proved to be the most thorough study ever carried out on the elimination of overlapping and the possible efficiency gains to be achieved through sovereignty. The work,

---

3. Unofficial translation: *Public Finance in a Sovereign Quebec, Sharing Canadian Government Assets and Debt, Study on the Administrative Restructuring of a Sovereign Quebec.*

carried out with the collaboration of all Quebec ministries, showed that annual saving would reach 2.7 billion dollars in 1995.[4]

The 1995 studies should be contextualized. Quebec's deficit was increasing so rapidly that, in the year 1994-95 when the Parti Québécois was returned to power, the deficit had reached a record six billion dollars. At the same time the federal government was attempting to reduce its own deficit, often at the expense of the provinces. It would have been possible to ensure that in a sovereign Quebec the new government would be able to provide the services formerly provided by the federal government, but that did not mean that it would be clear sailing. More specifically, as federal debt was increasing rapidly, the value of Quebec's share in the debt, which it must service, would automatically increase at the same time.

François Legault's accounting studies

François Legault's studies could not have been more timely. By 2005 the financial situation had changed entirely. Ottawa was afloat in surpluses while its debt had been substantially reduced, while Quebec had balanced its budget. François Legault outlined his approach as follows:

> In short, the study is an update of the *Analyse* pro forma *des finances publiques dans l'hypothèse de la souveraineté du Québec* (Pro forma analysis of public finances under the hypothesis of Quebec sovereignty) carried out in 1991 by the Secretariat of the Bélanger-Campeau Commission. [...] The study also updates the work done in 1995 by the Restructuration Secretariat as regards savings made through elimination of the overlapping. [...]
>
> Considering that the latest edition of the Public Accounts of Canada covers fiscal 2003-04, this study begins with an in-depth analysis of federal data for 2003-04 in order to establish Quebec's

---

4. François Legault, *Finances d'un Québec souverain*, p. 12. The three studies mentioned were published in 1995 by Les Publications du Québec, in the collection *"L'Avenir dans un Québec souverain."*

share of revenues and expenses. The data were then adjusted to 2005-06 in light of the 2005 federal budget estimates [...] Estimates for the next four years are provided. [...] Estimates on a five-year horizon for Quebec's revenues and expenses as a province are presented along with the revenues recovered from Ottawa and new expenses assumed by a sovereign Quebec.[5]

Once the objective and the methodology had been established, the results were validated by outside experts; collaboration with the administration in Quebec City and Ottawa was obtained in order to clarify certain issues. The results indicate the difference between revenues recovered from Ottawa and Quebec's expenditures needed to maintain those made by Ottawa in Quebec. Quebec's share of federal debt servicing is included and the cost of overlapping is gradually subtracted (over three years), namely the cost of duplicated administration (two income tax declarations rather than one, for instance). The net savings, which François Legault calls the "marge de manoeuvre" or leeway, are as follows (in millions of dollars):

2005-2006	1,324
2006-2007	1,503
2007-2008	2,843
2008-2009	3,638
2009-2010	4,500

It is clear that merging the operations of the Quebec government with those of the federal government in Quebec is profitable and that it is likely to become even more so with time. These figures may appear high, but it should be borne in mind that Quebec's GDP (gross domestic product) in 2009-10 is upwards of three hundred billion dollars. Predicting is hardly an exact science. The federal government, which for ten years beginning in 1995 drastically reduced transfer payments to provinces in order to balance its budget, then began to increase them significantly starting in 2007-08 to the point that, all other

---

5. *Ibid.*, pp. 12-13.

things being equal, the net savings built up almost vanished. In 2008, however, Ottawa announced that it would substantially reduce equalization payments to Quebec as of 2010-11, which should restore net savings.

But other factors had a greater impact. The financial crisis that broke out in 2008 and the recession that followed impacted the Ontario economy much more seriously than Quebec's, mainly because of its effect on the automobile industry. For the first time, the unemployment rate in Ontario exceeded that of its neighbour.[6] The federal government, the Ontario and Quebec governments announced several years of substantial budgetary deficits. The last time that the federal government faced a deficit of such magnitude, it cut transfer payments to provinces. Now, with Ontario joining the so-called "have-not" provinces eligible for equalization payments, Quebec faces the threat of reduced payments.

To sum up, it is clear that these accounting exercises could justify neither Quebec separation from Canada, nor its remaining a member of the Canadian federation. But they are by no means a waste of time. In fact, they demonstrate that equalization payments cannot be described as a gift from Canada to Quebec, which is perceived to be a "have-not" province, so that it can provide its own citizens with public services similar in quality to those provided by so-called rich provinces. Without these accounting exercises, it is impossible to reply to the argument that, without Canada, Quebec could not maintain its current standard of living.

Thanks to these complicated and often dry demonstrations, avowed federalist politicians have been heard to say on occasion that Quebec possesses the means to become an independent country. Recently, for example, Premier Jean Charest made a candid and unequivocal statement to this effect while on a state

---

6. Emploi-Québec, *L'emploi au Québec*, Newsletter, January 2009, p. 24, <http://emploiquebec.net/imt/emploi-au-quebec.asp>..

visit to Europe.[7] The population cannot be fooled either; after thirty-five years of highly technical debate and "battles of the balance sheet," it has the growing impression that can be summarized by the simple expression: "Yes, we can." As to whether it will be done, the Bloc Québécois polls mentioned in Chapter 4 are perfectly clear: a majority of Quebecers today do not believe that it will.

People have gradually become inured to the clash of figures; new objections have come to the fore. Using supposedly objective observations, obstacles that appear to be insurmountable are set up to impress and to discourage those who believe that an independent Quebec is not only possible but also desirable.

Expansion or decline? The "Lucids"

Two such conclusions have had a significant media impact. One of them can be summarized as follows: Quebec, along with Japan, has the most rapidly aging population in the world. Quebec's current population is a little more than 7.5 million; once it nudges over the eight million mark, it will begin to fall. In fifty years, the population of Quebec will be only a little greater than it is today.

The second depicts Quebec as the most indebted province in Canada, even deeper in debt than any state in the United States. "The bailiff is knocking."

So, here we are with a declining population, on the verge of bankruptcy. Yet we want to create our own country, which means we are either chasing mirages, or a living a pipedream. Thankfully Canada is always there—as we never cease being reminded—to support a failing Quebec state.

Among the papers published recently and written by those that I call the "declinologists," the clearest and most articulate is the brief entitled "Manifesto for a Clear-Sighted Vision (*Lucide*)

---

7. See *Le Devoir*, July 7, 2006, p. A3; *La Presse*, July 8, 2006, p. A2; July 11, 2006, p. A15.

of Quebec" whose signatories included a former Quebec premier, the editor-in-chief of a major daily newspaper, and three of Quebec's best-known economists. Here are some excerpts from the brief in the order in which they are presented.

Page 2: "From the financial standpoint, the Quebec government is like a heavy albatross that cannot take off; our per capita public debt is higher than anywhere on the continent. On the one hand, Quebec is about to experience the fastest demographic decline of all the industrialized countries except for Japan..."

Page 3: "Dreaming in Technicolour": "Some people are prepared to recognize certain of the problems that we have identified—our relative economic weakness in North America, our public debt, our demographic decline, the challenge from Asia. However, they believe and attempt to make the population believe that there are easy solutions to these problems, such as 'righting the fiscal imbalance' [...] Another solution advanced is Quebec sovereignty." While the signatories are not unanimous on this question, the title tells us all we need to know.

Page 4: "According to projections made by the *Institut de la statistique du Québec*, Quebec's population will be 7.8 million in 2050, a mere 300,000 more people than today. As early as 2012, there will be fewer and fewer people of working age, fewer and fewer young people, and more and more elderly. That will mean in turn a less dynamic, less creative, and less productive population [...]"

Page 6: "Within a few years, our dreams—in fact not our dreams but those of our children—will be brutally interrupted by bailiffs knocking at the door."

As a student in London in the early 1950s, I heard a saying that has always inspired me both as an economist and as a politician: "Statistics are to politics what lampposts are to drunkards: more for support than illumination."

The projections made by the *Institut de la statistique* used by the "clear-sighted" authors and other analysts and commentators predicting a decline in Quebec's population date back to 2003. [8] As with all demographic projections, they comprise three basic ingredients. First, the fertility rate, or the average number of children a woman will have while fertile. Without taking into account immigration and emigration, women must have an average of two children in order for population levels to be maintained (in fact it is a little more complicated and the factor of 2.1 is used). The second element is net immigration. For Quebec, the number of foreigners who enter, minus the number of Quebecers who leave Canada, is added to the number of residents of other provinces who come to Quebec, minus the number of Quebecers who leave for other provinces. The third element is life expectancy at birth. A longer life expectancy increases total population.

Predicting the future is never easy

L'Institut de la statistique du Québec drew up three projections based on hypotheses on fertility, net immigration, and life expectancy at birth: a low total population projection, a high projection, and a median projection that became the reference. In practice, everybody uses that reference projection.

The 2003 reference projection is based on a fertility rate of 1.5 (low: 1.3; high: 1.65), net immigration of 19,000 (low: 3,000; high: 35,000) and a life expectancy of 80.9 (for men) and 85.7 (for women) until 2025 and 84.5 and 88.6 respectively thereafter.

The population projections (in thousands) are as follows:

	Reference	Low	High
Population 2001	7,387	—	—
Population 2026	8,086	7,419	8,014
Population 2051	7,832	6,324	9,031

8. Institut de la statistique du Québec, *Si les tendances se maintiennent,* Perspectives démographiques, Québec et ses régions 2001-2051, p. 8.

The gap between high and low projections is enormous, almost fifty percent. In the absence of a political agenda or a doctrine, these figures should inspire caution. But dogmatists abhor nuance. If the goal is to demonstrate that Quebec is headed for the scrap-pile, then the reference scenario is brandished in order to "prove" the declining population of Quebec and all that necessarily follows.

On July 15, 2009, the *Institut de la statistique* published new population projections applicable for the period 2006-56. Family policies adopted by Quebec governments, particularly regarding subsidized daycare and parental leave, have had a demonstrable impact on fertility rates. An increase in net immigration and a drop in interprovincial emigration appear to have bolstered net immigration, while life expectancy at birth has continued to grow.

Here are the new hypotheses and new population projections:[9]

	Reference	Low	High
Fertility	1.65	1.5	1.85
Net immigration	30,000	14,000	46,000
Life expectancy M	85.5	83.3	88.0
Life expectancy W	89.0	86.3	90.5
Projected population (2056) (in thousands)	9,200	7,800	11,000

The situation has totally changed. It can no longer be argued that Quebec as a society is about to disappear or dissolve into a North American English-speaking world.

There remains one troublesome element, namely the record that Quebec supposedly shares with Japan regarding the rapidity with which the over-sixty-five age group is increasing. That image has been widely promoted; it should be corrected to take the most recent projections into account. There is some truth in the

---

9. Dominique André, *Perspectives démographiques du Québec et des régions 2006-2056,* Institut de la statistique du Québec, 2009. p. 20.

rapid aging phenomenon, but only in the first years, i.e., from 2001 to 2025, which reflects the astonishing drop in birthrates following the post-World War II baby boom. For the period 2025-2056, however, the aging rate in Quebec will likely remain below that of many other countries. "Statistics are to politics what lampposts are to drunkards..."

In the final analysis, like all developed countries Quebec has an aging population. Similarly, like most developed countries, Quebec can no longer rely on its birthrate to maintain its population and must take the necessary steps to support people having children, and open its doors to immigration to ensure its future. At the same time, immigrants must be able to integrate in ways that ensure that the host culture will survive and flourish. These are widespread concerns that by no means justify the alarm bells that some people enjoy ringing—quite unnecessarily.

Stabilizing public finances

Now, what about the debt? Early in the 1990s, Canada and Italy were the bad boys of the G7. Both had enormous annual deficits that made their debts skyrocket to the point that in 1996, thirty-eight cents out of each dollar of budgetary revenues went to service the debt (i.e., to pay interest). Ten years later, however, Canada had become the G7's pet, with recurrent budgetary surpluses, and a significantly reduced debt. In 2005, servicing of the debt represented no more than seventeen cents on each dollar.

Part of this remarkable financial turn-around was accomplished at the expense of the provinces that obviously passed on the responsibility to their own municipalities and school boards. However, it was impossible for the provinces to mine those budgets for what Ottawa had extracted from the provinces in the form of cuts to transfer payments.

Several provinces emerged from the 1990-91 recession with very significant deficits and the firm intention of balancing their budgets as quickly as they could. In some cases expenditures increased much more rapidly than sources of revenue, mainly in the health-care and education sectors. They could not rely on revenue sources like employment insurance, which became Ottawa's veritable cash cow. It can never be repeated often enough that the drastic reduction in accessibility to employment insurance is one of the main reasons the federal government was able to accumulate such large surpluses. Putting public finances in the provinces on an even keel was to prove a much more hazardous exercise.

The accounting rules mess

In 1996 Quebec set itself the same goal, but it began by setting draconian and ultimately unattainable conditions. As noted in Chapter 5, a zero deficit became the goal but it could be reached only by cutting costs; tax increases were ruled out; investments were to be made strictly in "cash." The goal proved impossible to attain without making extreme, and silly, cutbacks such as eliminating the highway construction budget. Some radical cutbacks were indeed made, particularly in hospital budgets, but taxes had to be raised and the accounting rules were changed. School taxes were increased in order to reduce school commission subsidies. Investments were no longer accounted for in the budget; only depreciation was to appear as an expense, with the amount invested being attributed directly to debt. Government revenues were made to include not only dividends paid by Hydro-Québec, but also all of the utility's profits, which henceforth transformed electricity rates into a tool for balancing the government's budget. But Hydro-Quebec's debt was not included even though the Quebec government guarantees it. These all may appear to be accounting tricks, but they have a serious impact on comparisons between the Ontario and Quebec debts. Indeed, at the end of 2007, the electricity sector in Ontario and Hydro-Québec had about the same level of debt, some thirty billion dollars. Hydro-Quebec, however, can boast assets of approximately sixty billion dollars, whereas those of the Ontario electricity sector amount to about twenty-three billion dollars, or less than the debt.

Hydro-Québec's balance sheet had the effect of reducing Quebec's total debt by thirty billion dollars, whereas Ontario's electricity sector increased that province's debt by seven billion. These figures, however, are not taken into account when the respective debts of the two governments are presented to the public,[10] but of course they are included in due diligence performed for Moody's or Standard and Poor's.

Once opened, the door to modified accounting rules is hard to close. The "generally accepted accounting principles" waltz is all but over. It has touched off some epic squabbles between the finance ministry and the auditor general. At one point the finance ministry stated that under Quebec's Balanced Budget Act, the 2005-06 accounts showed a surplus of 192 million, whereas the auditor general pointed to a deficit of 5.2 billion dollars.[11]

Debate over liabilities stemming from civil servants' pensions has been particularly acrimonious. For a long time, civil servants' pension contributions were considered as current government revenue, while pensions paid were expenses. During the Quiet Revolution, as long as the government was hiring more civil servants than were retiring, all went well. One day that would change however. In 1972, Quebec Finance Minister Raymond Garneau created a retirement fund for all new public sector employees (the RREGOP); contributions would be invested in the Caisse de dépôt et placement so that future commitments could be met. Something had to be done with the former teachers' and civil servants' funds in which the accumulated actuarial deficits were enormous. In my first budget speech in 1977, I announced

---

10. Data was obtained from the *Annual Report of the Ontario Electricity Financial Corporation*; the statements for Hydro One and Ontario Power Generation are included in Ontario's Public Accounts.

11. Vérificateur général du Québec, *Rapport spécial à l'Assemblée nationale concernant la vérification des états financiers consolidés pour l'année terminée le 31 mars 2006*, pp. 34-35.

that henceforth the depreciation of the actuarial deficit of those funds and the accruing interest would be considered as expenses. No other province had acted to face future actuarial commitments. Raymond Garneau and I laid the groundwork.

Debate with auditors general about the "Quebec formula" has gone on for years. As usual, the auditors always end up winning. Their victory was complete in 1997 when twenty billion dollars, including fifteen billion dollars in retirement pensions were added to the Quebec debt, which, as it was then calculated, stood at seventy-eight billion dollars. Other changes were then introduced, though less significant. Another accounting reform was carried out in 2007, but this time school commission and health-care service finances were included, adding twenty billion dollars to the debt.

I will only mention here the inclusion of the financial commitments of the Quebec workmen's compensation commission (CSST; Commission de la santé et de la sécurité au Travail) into Quebec government accounts, followed by its expulsion a few years later.

After all of this sleight of hand, the task of analysing Quebec's debt and of comparing it with others is a tricky one indeed. Certain comparative tables are very strange indeed. For example, in the 2009-10 Finance Ministry's so-called "Plan budgétaire," pension liabilities add thirty billion dollars to Quebec's debt, whereas the same budget item represents fourteen billion dollars for all the other provinces combined... And in Ontario, pension liabilities are replaced by assets in the amount of 3.7 billion dollars.[12]

Debate on the debt

For all of these reasons, it is no surprise that debate about Quebec's debt has become so shrill. The debate turned truly acrimonious in the wake of the 1997 accounting reforms, when

---

12. Québec, ministère des Finances, plan budgétaire 2009-2010, p. D14

the debt reached one hundred billion dollars. In the years that followed, nobody could explain why the debt kept growing while the budget deficit was consistently zero. In 2006 the debt was close to one hundred and twenty billion, the following year it soared up to one hundred and forty-three billion.[13] Faced with this gargantuan figure, budgetary documents indicated that the "new" favourite measurement of the debt would be the one represented by accumulated deficits. Thus the figure dropped below the one hundred billion mark. Since Ontario and Alberta do it that way, it must be right.

This type of manipulation ends up affecting both journalistic commentary and the general public; it also influences those who set policy and make decisions. Two finance ministers used the expression "the bailiffs are knocking." If they really think so, one wonders what impact that belief has on them while they are preparing their budgets?

The Quebec government, school commissions, municipalities, government-owned corporations (particularly Hydro-Quebec), hospitals, and universities form, from the financial standpoint, a system of communicating vessels. Revenues for one can be increased by reducing resources provided to the other, with the government determining how each branch of the Quebec public sector will share resources. Moreover, each province establishes its own method for sharing resources. Depending on how deficits are shared, borrowing is likewise shared. What counts in the long run is that all borrowing for the public sector goes towards paying for public sector investments, and not to pay day-to-day expenses (i.e., paying the grocery bill). Borrowing to invest and build is perfectly normal.[14]

---

13. *Ibid.*, p. D11.
14. During recessions, of course, some borrowing is required for current expenses, but it must be reimbursed during periods of prosperity.

Comparisons with the OECD: Quebec is normal

For at least thirty years (to the best of my recollection), budgetary documents compare public sector borrowings and investments in face-to-face tables. In recent years, it was becoming harder and harder to insist that "the bailiffs are knocking." The situation was simply too normal. For the year 2003-04, public sector borrowing represented only forty-eight percent of investments, which meant that more than half of investments were financed by current revenues. The situation was so normal that it was intolerable. It was thus decided that budgetary documents would delete the table presenting public sector investments. Only the table of amounts borrowed was presented. No longer was it possible to show how normal Quebec was. "Statistics are to politics what lampposts..."

But how do Quebec and Canada compare with other countries? The best basis for comparison available is the OECD, to which the most industrialized countries belong. The method established for comparing public debt consists in presenting the entire public sector of each country, including public pension plans (such as Quebec's pension plan, La Régie des rentes), but without government employee pension plan liabilities. Assets are subtracted from liabilities.[15] The results available apply to 2006, before the financial and economic crisis changed the picture.

To align Quebec's data with OECD data, it is assumed that Quebec is independent and assuming full responsibility for its share of federal debt.[16] For the rest, the same calculation methods used by the OECD are applied to Quebec data. The results are as follows:

---

15. Data base *OECD Economic Outlook No. 82.*
16. The method used was the one proposed by the Bélanger-Campeau Commission.

	Net Public Indebtedness 2006 (% of GDP)
Germany	60.2
OECD Average	46.9
United States	46.5
United Kingdom	43.4
France	43.4
Quebec	30.9
Canada	20.0

The table illustrates how remarkably Canada's financial situation had improved, and, moreover, continues to improve. The previous year, public indebtedness stood at 29.9 percent, and the OECD predicted that it would be fifteen percent in 2007. The recent crisis will undoubtedly push the percentages back up, but that will be the case for the other countries too.

Quebec is surely more in debt than Canada, but its rate is so much lower than the average OECD rate that it is hard to understand what people are so frightened about. As a province, Quebec seems constantly to be the focus of anxiety, undoubtedly blown out of proportion, sometimes willfully; this anxiety also unquestionably influences how governments perceive the present and fear the future. As a country, Quebec would have no particular reason to be afraid or to allow others to frighten it.

Chapter 8

THE QUEBEC STATE

It can never be said often enough: an independent Quebec would mean that Quebecers will have the power to determine their laws, taxes and the treaties that link them with other countries. A highly centralized state fully assumes these three functions and delegates the day-to-day administration of its policies and programs to local entities (municipalities, school boards, regions, etc.). In a federation, each of the members has, theoretically at least, sovereign powers over certain activities or jurisdictions. In a unitary state, all local or regional powers are delegated and the central government can modify them as it sees fit. Delegation can take several forms. When the responsibility for carrying out activities is delegated, it is deconcentration. If what is delegated is the power to make decisions, hire, raise taxes, and devise programs within flexible or rigid standards, then it is decentralization. Deconcentration and decentralization come in all shapes and sizes. That is why the unrestrained use of the term "decentralization" has the effect of diluting its meaning. When abstract terms are not defined, it is difficult to determine exactly what they mean. Quebecers often decry the degree of centralization of the federal government. Yet from a fiscal standpoint, the Canadian federation is one of the most decentralized in the world, while from a legal standpoint, it is quite the opposite. Since these are abstract terms when they are not clearly put in context, I will try to be as concrete as possible.

Many of the questions raised in this section will have to be decided one day by a Constituent Assembly. Many points of view will be expressed on how the Quebec state will be organized; obviously, I have no way of knowing what decisions will be made. The following are simply my own views on some of these questions.

What type of political system?

The first question would be to determine what type of political system do people want for Quebec. First of all, would an independent Quebec remain a monarchy or would it become a republic? The answer is, I think, obvious. Quebecers are not convinced monarchists, to put it mildly. Becoming a republic will, I think, be a very natural development, with a president replacing the Queen's representative.

This brings us to a more complicated question, namely what political system would Quebec adopt? To different degrees, Quebecers are familiar with three systems. First, we have grown familiar with the British system ever since a form of parliamentary government was granted to us in 1791. Our system has evolved here just as it has in London, yet it remains today similar to that of the former colonial power. The king (thereafter the president) reigns but does not govern. The head of the party with the most elected members of parliament governs. In the American system the president holds executive power and governs. The president's powers appear to be immense but, in fact, they are balanced by those held by Congress. There is no prime minister and the president appoints cabinet members, who report to him, from among people not elected to Congress. The role of the president in France is a compromise between these two systems. The French system resembles the British one in that the prime minister and the cabinet are appointed from among the elected members of the National Assembly, but the powerful role played by the president puts him in a similar position to that of the president of the United States. He is responsible for national defence and foreign affairs and can change the prime minister or dissolve parliament when he so wishes.

Sovereigntists often debated these issues intensely in the past. The French system in particular, symbolized by the preeminent personality of General de Gaulle, was very attractive, whereas the simple fact that our old existing system was British was enough to make it much less interesting.

Time has passed. I think Quebecers today are more interested in making improvements to the system they live in than in changing it. My opinion has always been that it is better to have an imperfect system that we know and can amend than to seek out perfection that can take years to master. The French have proven to be remarkably versatile on this point. Since 1791, they have gone through five republics, two empires and two monarchies. That has given them a capacity to adapt that we could never imitate. We're just as well off keeping what we know.

That does not mean that the present system cannot be improved. Pressure has become very strong for the introduction of a certain degree of proportional representation in elections to the Quebec parliament. In our one-time, first-past-the-post electoral system the person with the most votes is elected even when, owing to the number of candidates, she or he might only represent thirty-five percent of votes cast. Odd things have been known to occur. For instance, in 1973, the Parti Québécois won thirty percent of the popular vote but only six seats out of a total of one hundred and ten, yet it still became the Official Opposition in Quebec.

Proportional representation

Such oddities are inherent in our electoral system and they can be avoided by adopting a system of proportional representation. Each party presents a list of candidates for all National Assembly seats. Let us say one hundred seats in all. One party obtains fifteen percent of the votes cast. It will thus have fifteen elected members, namely the first fifteen names on the party's list. The same applies to the other parties. It is a perfectly fair system, which would obviously lead to the creation of many new parties. If a movement for the protection of canaries obtained two percent of votes cast, it would be assigned two seats. That can lead to a high degree of instability for governments since the parties must continually negotiate and renegotiate alliances as soon as one or two parties withdraw causing the government to fall.

One corrective would be to establish a rule under which a party must obtain a minimum of five percent of votes cast in order to participate in power-sharing negotiations.

Proportional representation, however, makes it impossible for voters to vote for "their" representative. This is not a consideration to be sneezed at. In 1984, René Lévesque asked a group of ministers to study the system of proportional representation. We were all surprised to see the extent to which voters believed it important to vote directly for a particular individual, and not simply for a party. This could be partially remedied, of course, by establishing regional lists and dividing up the seats according to the performance of each party in each region. However, that does not really satisfy the voter who wants to pass judgment on "his" or "her" representative.

Finally, the list electoral system has one major disadvantage, a crippling one in my opinion. The secretary general or the leader of the party is responsible for drawing up that party's list, and by the same token, for appointing members. That means that the party decides who will be elected. A candidate with a reputation as a free thinker will never appear high on the list. In a sense, the party's secretary general replaces the voter.

It must also be said that voters can make mistakes. Political parties that strive to be very democratic have their candidates chosen by the members of riding associations. This inevitably leads to the kind of situation in which an elected member's assistant, who has devoted perhaps fifteen years to the "cause," who is known by everybody and who controls the list of party members, has a jump on another very good candidate, potentially a cabinet minister, but who cannot resign from his or her job six or eight months before the election to campaign among party members. The second person is likely to lose out to the party bureaucrat, who may be much younger and has only half the experience and public profile. That often happened when I was leader of the Parti Québécois, and for that reason I particularly admire the formula developed in Germany after World War II that, sixty years later, is still used and has often been imitated.

In Quebec today, that would mean that seventy-five out of the 125 members of the National Assembly, would continue to represent their ridings directly. The electoral ridings could be those that apply in federal elections, with some adjustments made to take account of Ungava in the north and the Îles-de-la-Madeleine in the Gulf of St. Lawrence.

Fifty seats would be allotted based on regional proportional representation. The political parties could thus appoint certain candidates whom they believe must be elected, while, for the small parties that, under the existing system, only manage to reach the National Assembly by chance, the formula would make it possible for them to be elected if they obtain a given percentage of the votes cast in the region in which they run. People should not be surprised that the number of seats in the Quebec National Assembly is limited to one hundred and twenty-five. In fact, that is the building's current capacity. Any sizeable increase in the number of elected representatives would require the construction of a new building, and that might be difficult to justify.

An upper house? Representing regions?

Would an independent Quebec have a single house of assembly? Canada, like many countries, has always had a senate in addition to the House of Commons. One house has decision-making power and is the basic entity since it is the expression of the people's will, while the other often has the power only to propose amendments and to return bills to the first house, without being able to block the expression of the people's will. It is the chamber for "sober second thoughts." In political systems that stem from the British model, the second house is not elected, but appointed, as in the case of Canada's Senate. Since political organizers and friends of the regime in power tend to pack these second houses, they have lost much of their lustre. It is another story altogether in countries where the upper house is elected through universal suffrage. Of all the formulas used, the most interesting in my opinion would be to make the upper house into an assembly of the regions. The astonishingly rapid development of large urban areas combined with the danger of a continued exodus from rural and forest areas makes it extremely useful to be able to assess the impact of legislation and budget programs on the regions, while still recognizing the primacy of the National Assembly and the necessity of treating all the country's citizens equally. It would appear wise, in my opinion, to ensure a balance between the regions and the conurbations of Quebec City and Montreal, without however preventing the will of the people from being fully expressed.

Judging by the number of foreign examples, many formulas are possible. The Constituent Assembly will have to decide. For purposes of debate, I will hazard a suggestion.

A second house, that could be called the Assembly of Regions, would comprise the same number of representatives as would be elected directly by the ridings, namely seventy-five. Montreal would have fewer seats than would be justified by the island's population, and not more than a quarter of the seats available. The smaller regions would have a guaranteed minimum number of seats, perhaps three or four. These would all be elected positions.

This assembly would be responsible for studying the regional impact of legislation and budgets. It could propose amendments to the National Assembly on everything that has a direct impact on regions. But it would also wield veto power over legislation dealing with certain essential aspects of life in the regions, such as budgets for universities other than those in Montreal and Quebec City, owing particularly to the increasing impact of higher education and research on regional growth. Another such example would be the budgetary allotments for regional radio and television production. Many other examples can be considered, particularly in the discussion below about what I identify as the devolution of powers and resources to local and regional authorities in an independent Quebec.

Transition measures will be required. For example, it would be useful to draw on the experience acquired by Quebec's members of parliament in Ottawa in areas in which the Quebec National Assembly has little or no expertise. Those elected parliamentarians might well become the first members of the Assembly of Regions; when the first general election is called, they could run for either of the assemblies. This of course is only a suggestion among others.

Critical to the success of this operation is bridging the gap between Montreal and the rest of Quebec, reducing the apprehension in remote regions that they will lose all their young people and their future, and provide them with means to defend themselves. This is a common problem in our day. All small countries (in terms of population) seek to strike a balance between their large cities, which are their political or economic capitals, and outlying regions. Quebec does not need to be independent to reestablish this balance. Indeed, nothing today prevents Quebec from adopting its own constitution, one that would establish a second house. In fact, Quebec had one until 1968, known as the Legislative Council, which was the provincial equivalent of the Canadian Senate. Quebec could have reformed it but chose to eliminate it instead. Quebec has the power, as a province, to have its own constitution as long as it does not touch the position of lieutenant governor, or more accurately, the monarchy.

If Quebec were to create a second house tomorrow, some of the powers mentioned above would not be available, such as regulating radio and television, which would remain a federal jurisdiction. Should Quebec adopt its own constitution, the Canadian Constitution would remain simultaneously in force.

The temptation to centralize

Quebec independence would produce a completely new financial situation. Among the many decisions that the government will have to make in the wake of a referendum victory, those touching on finance are likely to prove spectacular. For example, all employers will be informed that as of a given date income taxes deducted at source are to be sent to Quebec City rather than to Ottawa. Similarly, GST payments will be kept in Quebec. In fact, all income and other taxes that Quebecers currently pay to the federal government would be paid to the Quebec government, a measure that would almost double budgetary revenues.[1] Quebec would of course assume responsibility from the beginning for all expenses that are now Ottawa's responsibility. Municipal and school taxes would then account for no more than ten percent of public sector revenues. Quebec would become a centralized country whose government would be responsible for almost everything. That in turn would undoubtedly be good for democracy: the citizen and the voter will always know who is responsible for what, which is certainly not the case now. The federal and provincial governments are in bitter competition, to the point that it is impossible in the end to establish who is responsible, be it for the areas where everything seems to work well or those that cause problems. What's more, there is so much duplication that billions of dollars are wasted, as was shown in the Chapter 7.

But a government that does almost everything, however, is

---

1. Federal government transfers will of course halt.

inefficient. If it must administer everything, it will do so badly, if not much worse. In Quebec, we already tend to blame the minister for even the smallest incident. Anybody who follows question period in the National Assembly will realize that debate is burdened by details that never should reach such a level. It's as if the mayor, police chief, school principal or hospital manager were merely steps that lead to the National Assembly member, often ending up in the responsible minister's lap or, if unavailable, with one of the minister's representatives.

Human nature will not change and we must learn to live with it. Nonetheless, in organizing the state, it is necessary to devise a formula that ensures efficiency, and can be measured by the quality and speed with which services are provided to the population.

What to decentralize?

This issue should be widely debated. Until now, each time decentralization has made it onto the political agenda, only marginal issues are discussed. The province already has a hard time balancing its books; it has little or no money to transfer to local authorities, and it can only transfer very limited responsibilities. Citizens are not fooled when the government, instead of increasing taxes, "devolves" substantial responsibilities, forcing municipalities to raise property taxes.

In an independent Quebec the situation would be entirely different. The central government would exercise national responsibilities, including international relations, national defence and internal security. As I have shown, it would possess far more resources and would be in a position to transfer to the local level both local responsibilities and the resources to deal with them. In addition to primary and secondary education, local clinics or CLSCs, long-term care and housing facilities, social housing, sports and recreation, and cultural activities, to name but a few, can be decentralized. Decentralization of certain services can be complete, with the government keeping responsibility only for establishing standards and monitoring the quality of training and services but exercising no administrative responsibility. Decentralization can also be partial. For example, collective bargaining for teachers or hospital personnel can be decentralized, except for wage scales and other major monetary issues.

We can safely assert that any increase in municipal and regional financial resources will generate many economic development initiatives, investment incentives and industrial promotion.

Transfer of resources need not necessarily take the form of government subsidies to local authorities. Once the Quebec government controls its share of federal income taxes collected, as well as the integrated Quebec sales tax and federal goods and services tax, substantial reductions in income tax and goods and services tax rates will be in order so that local authorities will be able to establish their own income tax rates and sales taxes. This may surprise some, but it is how things work in several American states where municipalities have the right to determine their own income tax rate and to apply their own sales taxes. Many municipalities take advantage of such provisions. New York City, for instance, has a progressive income tax that does not exceed four percent, but it applies a 4.5-percent sales tax. Many cities have established lower sales taxes of one or two percent to avoid chasing shoppers away.

Another formula consists in reserving a predetermined share of sales taxes for all municipalities. Since wealthier cities can collect larger amounts than poorer cities, an equalization system can be devised to ensure equitable distribution. Though it may appear complicated, this formula was applied for years in Quebec before 1980.

In my capacity both as chair of a commission studying the future of Quebec municipalities and as leader of the Parti Québécois, discussion of these issues with municipal mayors was always fraught with difficulty. Local officials probably saw them as unrealistic and theoretical. As long as a referendum on sovereignty has not been won, raising such issues will continue to be difficult. But when the exercise becomes credible, it will be clear that many formulas for decentralization, responsibility and resource-sharing formulas exist and are applied throughout the world. It is striking to note that even in traditionally centralized countries like France decentralization has grown by leaps and bounds over the last twenty years. Sometimes echoes of this change reach us. The Scandinavian countries, whose populations are similar to Quebec's, are a case in point. Their education ministries have between two and three hundred civil servants. How can that be? say we, with our fifteen hundred-plus knowledge and education bureaucrats. Yet the trend is there, solid and entirely consistent with the principle that government works best when it is closest to the people it serves, in addition to making good sense.

Cities or regions?

Until now, my use of the term *local authorities* has been purposefully vague. We, in Quebec, are interested in structures, which we have substantially modified since the Quiet Revolution without ever really clarifying the role of regions. In fact, our focus has been mainly on municipalities—some might even call it obsession.

Quebec's regions and regional capitals were created as administrative structures in 1965. It was done at a time when we were impressed by France's sweeping planning methods and did not understand that planning is an illusion when you only have responsibility for half of your public resources and when most large corporations report to another government. Yet the 1965 effort had the positive effect of providing guidelines for the establishment of public administration that reported to the Quebec government.

Several administrative regions corresponded to real areas in which people had a sense of belonging. These included the

Abitibi-Témiscamingue, Saguenay-Lac-Saint-Jean, Bas-du-Fleuve, and Gaspésie regions. In other areas, it was not quite so clear, but the administrative decision did succeed in strengthening cohesion, as was the case with the Mauricie and Estrie (or Eastern Townships) regions. Defining regional administrative areas in the Montreal area was much more arbitrary. The surrounding areas could just as well have been divided up by drawing concentric circles around Montreal Island rather than drawing pieces of pie pointing to the centre, which begin with bedroom suburbs and reach out to forested regions in the Upper Laurentians.

Over time people became accustomed to the structure. Some changes were made: the Gaspé region was separated from the Lower St. Lawrence, for example. On the whole, the organization has stood the test of time and gradually the administration adapted itself. Regional structures sprang up in health-care services, cultural councils, and so on.

No political umbrella structure was developed for regions, however, while municipal structures evolved rapidly. Urban communities had formed to allow municipalities in the large centres to pool their efforts in areas of shared responsibility. The creation of regional county municipalities (MRCs) in 1979 represented a major innovation, setting up an efficient, modern land-use instrument based on the old county-based structure that had become obsolete. All the municipal mayors are members of the MRC for which they elect a prefect. They also share the cost of any initiatives they may undertake. A local financial instrument designed to support small businesses and employment, known as *sociétés locales d'investissement dans le développement de l'emploi* (SOLIDE), was set up. Certain public services were reorganized along the lines of the MRCs, such as the local health clinics or CLSCs, even though authority remains with the regional agency and the health and social services ministry.

What powers for the regions?

The accent has remained on the local authority, namely the municipality (strengthened by municipal mergers) and to a lesser degree on school authorities, while the regions enjoy none of the attributes of real government.

Problems arise when it comes to transferring resources, areas of taxation and responsibilities. They can be counted upon to touch off sharp debate, especially if the idea of an Assembly of Regions is finally adopted. If the people who represent regions have effective decision-making powers on questions such as regional radio and television or regional university budgets, then administrative and decision-making structures will be required; in other words, a political authority to which administrators will report. It will be important however not to "over-administer" the new independent Quebec.

In my opinion, the municipal structure should continue to be the principle one. I agree that opinions will diverge. Mayors keep the regions operating, but they obviously need help from representatives of the civil society.

Two conditions must be met in order for this scheme to work. First, a substantial share of resources should take the form of taxation rather than subsidies, with the Quebec government determining in advance how much of its own fiscal base it is prepared to relinquish. Secondly, while meeting standards set by the government, cities must be in a position to take initiatives, devise programs, and determine how much of their resources they wish to devote to them. This degree of autonomy would alter the roles of both mayors and city councils. An effective mayor will no longer be the one who manages to pump the most money out of the federal and Quebec governments. A good mayor will be the person who says: "The new concert hall, stadium or whatever else is going to cost so much. I propose to pay for half of it with our income taxes and the other half with a loan that will cost us so much a year. Do you agree?" The government's role with regard to municipalities (other than setting of standards of course) would be limited to ensuring equalization between rich and poor cities.

Such a formula would help solve the second serious problem arising from the presence of increased resources in the hands of local authorities. Public debate would be more meaningful when local authorities propose large investment projects; participation in local elections should increase as well. It is hard to imagine doubling the funds available for local authorities and allowing them to use it as they see fit without first making sure that democratic processes are respected. Otherwise, the door would be open for the creation of personal fiefdoms ruled by patronage, nepotism, and corruption.

A clear-cut Constitution

We have drifted away from constitutional issues; we must now return to them. On the basis of the preceding pages, it should come as no surprise that the new Quebec Constitution would not have a federal structure. It will be based on the Quebec Charter of Rights and Freedoms; the state, which proceeds from the sovereignty that the people have bestowed upon it, will organize Quebec society. Sovereignty will not be dispersed. The Constitution must clearly set forth the powers to be wielded by the head of state, the head of government, and to each of the houses (if the principle of two houses is adopted) and to the courts. In like manner, the Constitution must be explicit about rights, particularly regarding equality before the law. This is not always a simple matter. Many rights have been recognized with respect to the English community and the Aboriginal peoples, and new rights with regard to religion are appearing, in the name of reasonable accommodation, that sometimes go beyond the notion of freedom of belief and religion.

Decisions will have to be made about what must be, what can be, and what should absolutely not be included in the Quebec

Constitution. Care must also be taken to devise an appropriate amending formula. The goal of Quebec sovereignty is to bring government and citizens closer to one another. Even though the goal is not a new one, it is a major innovation considering the magnitude of the changes that must be made. Time will be needed to experiment with different systems before casting them in constitutional stone.

It will be imperative that when citizens cast their votes they know that the responsibilities to be exercised by the people they elect have been clearly established. In our day, image making has become such a dominant consideration that, despite the spin and mystification, citizens must be clearly aware of who does what and how it is done.

Chapter 9

THE SECRET OF GROWTH

Natural resources have long been long been cited as the principal reason for Quebec's economic growth. The narrative begins with the beaver, goes on to forestry and mining, then hydropower. It took a very long time to recognize that the most precious of all our natural resources is the population's grey matter.

It has been long believed that industrial development required trade barriers of different kinds to protect industries whose main market was Canada and whose costs would often be higher than the corresponding American industries that benefitted from a much larger domestic market. Canada, and of course Quebec, exported raw materials and sought to expand the range of manufactured goods by protecting them against foreign competition.

That is all history now; the picture has changed with the expansion of free trade. We have come to understand that the capacity to export goods, based on productivity and innovation, determines prosperity levels. The more trade is liberalized throughout the world, the more acutely we understand the consequences and the applications of this principle. It also holds true irrespective of what political status we might choose, be it the Free Republic of Sept-Îles, an independent Quebec, or a united Canada.

No country is too small to prosper and to enjoy an acceptable growth rate as long as two conditions are met. It must have access to a large market and its businesses must be competitive. Europe has taught us that lesson and has demonstrated it for the past fifty years. Being competitive comprises two elements: productivity, which means efficiency or the capacity to sell at a price equal to or lower than that of competitors, and innovation, or the ability to put new and different goods or services on the market that correspond to, or create, demand.

Productivity

Productivity is measured by production per hour of work. It has nothing to do with the number of hours worked in a week or in a year. In one country, people may work fewer hours a week but, thanks to high hourly productivity, that country remains very competitive. For many goods and services, the capacity to export is a good productivity indicator. If we can sell our goods internationally, we can probably protect ourselves against imports. To maintain such a situation, productivity must continually be improving as other countries are likewise working to enhance their own productivity. Should our productivity lag, selling goods on the international market will become increasingly difficult and other countries will flood our own market, which in turn will drive domestic production down, cause lay-offs, and other adverse effects.

Many goods and services never cross borders, but productivity in these areas also contributes to the country's prosperity. For instance, we can still imagine a time when snow was removed with shovels and brooms. Applied to today's situation, that would mean either an army of snow-removers paid very low wages or sky-high property taxes for everyone, or some of both. The example is obviously preposterous but it illustrates that in areas such as the public sector, which are not exposed to market pressures, productivity must also continually improve. While a business that fails to increase its productivity will sooner or later be overtaken by competitors, a public administration that does the same runs only the risk, sooner or later, of being defeated in the political arena.

Between the public administration and a business trying to thrive in a global economy, are a multitude of small businesses with local markets and local competition that avoid categorization—except that the owners' and employees' incomes will depend on their productivity, their work and, in many cases, on their capacity to innovate.

The main way to increase productivity is to invest in equipment, machinery, information technologies, and production management. For years economic textbooks taught that if developed countries that paid high salaries were able to compete with countries where wages were low, it was because the former had sophisticated equipment handled by a much more qualified workforce.

That is less and less the case. Computerized technologies, for much standardized production, are considerably more productive than any other combination of less sophisticated equipment run by a little-trained workforce, and so there is really no alternative. As a result, industrial sectors in so-called emerging countries are now just as well equipped technologically as the so-called developed countries, in addition to boasting lower wages. But as time passes and productivity increases wages also rise, which prompts companies to seek out lower wages elsewhere. Japanese companies provide the perfect illustration. They first grew because they combined high tech with low wages. When Japanese wages rose to European and North American levels, Japanese businesses shifted production to other places in Southeastern Asia in order to keep growing. This had been understood for years in Western Europe and North America. In some of these countries, whole industries simply disappeared.

Innovation

Increasing productivity alone cannot ensure growth in modern economies. Innovation is also required. Goods and services do not sell only because the price is low; they also have special features that make them unique and attractive. The term *innovation* must be taken with its full meaning, such as research for a new form of a conventional product, better quality goods or new trends. It can take the form of a particular use of a conventional product, development of a new material or process to cut costs or improve quality; or it can be a medical discovery, new software, artistic or intellectual creation, or a new product that nobody had ever thought of before. Innovation is in some ways a state of mind.

Innovation can be found everywhere. For instance, it can be the decision to manufacture two helicopter models for the world market at Mirabel or the introduction of a peat-bagging machine near Rivière-du-Loup. Innovation encompasses the reinventing of the circus by the Cirque du Soleil, Ubisoft's video-game software or the development or a new derivative at what's left of the Montreal Stock Exchange. The list goes on indefinitely, encompassing new products and new services that appear and replace those that disappear. These goods and services spring from the R&D departments of huge corporations, like the new motors in the Bombardier C Series, but also from basements and garages, particularly in computers and information technologies.

Innovation and productivity are the two keys to growth and prosperity. As such, they must lie at the heart of any government's economic policies. This was not so clear when governments had instruments they could use to set goals within borders that protected them, but globalization has changed everything. I remember one keynote speaker telling members of the Chicoutimi Chamber of Commerce a few years ago, "Make no mistake about it, somebody somewhere, perhaps in Korea or Taiwan, is working to put you out of business."

How are these two poles of economic growth faring in Quebec? As a whole, productivity in Quebec is about ten percent behind that of Canada, which in turn is about fifteen percent behind that of the United States.[1] Gaps of this magnitude have existed for a long time and tend not to be reduced. They are averages that conceal much more complex situations. For example, when Quebec industries are classified according to their degree of technological advancement in the four categories of activities established by the OECD, Quebec belongs to the highest (owing to the aeronautical, pharmaceutical and IT industries), but nowhere else is there such a high proportion of fourth category industries (i.e., the least technologically advanced industries).[2]

The Centre de recherche industrielle du Québec (CRIQ) made a particularly interesting diagnosis based on a study of 1,200 companies conducted in 2002. "Quebec manufacturing companies invest less than their neighbours to the south in high tech production equipment. Secondly, they only have a limited understanding of the competitive environment. And finally, few of them have an integrated production chain management approach."[3]

Companies of this kind are vulnerable to competition, whether from the rest of Canada or from the United States. In addition, the exchange rate must be factored into all commercial transactions with the United States. Since an independent Quebec will keep the Canadian dollar, what applies today will apply as well in future.

---

1. These are approximations. For example, see *Assessing Quebec's Key Prosperity and Competitiveness Opportunities and Challenges* by Claude Séguin (Institute for Competitiveness and Prosperity, February 2007).
2. Centre de recherche industrielle du Québec, le CRIQ. *Un instrument incontournable pour l'amélioration de la productivité dans les industries liées au secteur des ressources*, 2001, p. 16.
3. Serge Guérin, CEO of the CRIQ, open letter published in *La Presse*, May 1, 2002.

Anesthesia

Between 2003 and 2006, the value of the Canadian dollar rose forty percent against the United States dollar, as well as the Chinese Yuan, directly impacting the Quebec and Ontario economies. For some thirty years the exchange rate had masked the growing productivity gap between the United States and Canada. It had acted like an anesthetic. Canada and Quebec remained competitive on the United States market because the value of the Canadian dollar gradually, but irregularly, fell against that of the United States. Modernizing equipment became increasingly costly as governments failed to offset the negative impact with grants and fiscal incentives. One might have thought that as the Canadian dollar grew in strength, driving down the price of imported goods, investments in production facilities and machinery would have increased strongly. In fact, they only grew modestly.

When the 2008 financial crisis led to widespread recession, it might also have been expected that the impact on the manufacturing industry would have been more acute. Once again, the exchange rate came to the rescue. As oil prices floundered, the value of the Canadian dollar fell by twenty percent against its US counterpart thus limiting the damage that lack of foresight might have caused. Whether Quebec remains part of Canada or becomes independent, there is one problem that we understand very well and have attempted several times to remedy but with little success, one that must be addressed much more energetically and imaginatively.

Innovation cannot be measured with instruments similar to those used to measure productivity per hour worked. Counting registered patents does not mean much since patents are registered in Ottawa and in any case many of those originating in Quebec, or in Canada for that matter, are registered directly in the United States. It is interesting, however, to track the curve of investment in research and development, and to compare it with other countries. In this area, Quebec's performance has improved significantly.

Progress in research and development

Total research and development investment in Quebec, expressed as a percentage of GDP, has increased substantially. In fact, such investments in Quebec exceed those in the rest of Canada and compare favourably with many other countries. In short, Quebec is not a "problem case" as it was until some twenty years ago. It has now caught up. Overall figures however only provide impressions. Several very large corporations are responsible for a major share of private sector research and development. For small and medium-size businesses, the situation is so diversified and complex that generalizations cannot be made. For many businesses operating with new technologies, research is the starting point. Indeed, the business only comes into being when research results prove promising; companies are frequently sold even before they can bring a new product to market.

But for many other small and medium-size businesses, the main contact with research and development takes place when they acquire advanced technologies and new management systems, which usually have more impact on productivity than on innovation. Generally speaking, the more dynamic the businesses, the quicker it is to adopt new techniques; others tend to lag behind. Government support programs must take these disparities into account.

The question of government support for businesses must be addressed. From the perspective of an independent Quebec, we must first clarify our ideas and goals, then dust off and reorganize the tools in our toolbox. Many modifications are possible within the Canadian context; others can only be addressed in the context of an independent Quebec, whatever the form of association to be established with Canada and the United States.

Clarifying our ideas and goals is more difficult than meets the eye. Some people believe that the government's role is mainly to establish a user-friendly fiscal system for businesses and provide quality schooling and university training. When these conditions are met, according to conventional wisdom, market forces will determine who will, or will not, discover a promising new product or service, then produce it better at a lower price than the competition.

Intervention is necessary

What is irritating about this outlook is that it draws on two healthy principles—quality education and competitive taxation—and then transforms them into exclusion and dogmatism. Never before have economies been transformed so rapidly and in such a global manner. These movements are of such magnitude that even the most conservative governments are forced by public opinion to intervene massively to ensure the economy will keep functioning. The 2007-08 financial crisis has provided the most overwhelmingly negative demonstration imaginable. Deregulation of financial institutions, starting in the United States, but applied almost everywhere and carried out in the name of the economic model described above, engendered massive indebtedness based on new financial products (derivatives) and unprecedented risk-taking. The subprime mortgage crisis in the United States triggered a financial crisis that caused enormous losses, estimated at some four trillion dollars by the International Monetary Fund for financial institutions alone. [4] Quebec incurred its own share of those losses, with the Caisse de dépôt et placement alone registering a drop of forty billion dollars, or one percent of all losses worldwide.

Loss in turn forced banks to reduce commercial credit, which inevitably triggered a recession. The recession in turn led to the

---

4. The resistance of the Canadian banking system during this meltdown deserves to be mentioned.

failure of two of the major United States automobile manufac-
turers that had become increasingly unable to meet the competition, mainly from Japan, on the one hand because of their costs
(bloated by the cost of pensions and health-care plans) and on
the other because of their very conservative car and business
models.

Did the government of the United States have a choice? Could
it allow the financial catastrophe to take its course and simply
wash its hands of any responsibility for the collapse of a major
sector of the American economy? Obviously it could not, just as
the other countries in the world could not avoid intervening in
an attempt to limit the damage resulting from a financial crisis
that rapidly went global, and to jump start their own national
economies without turning to protectionism or avoiding it as
much as possible.

They didn't use kid gloves. Simply to see the United States
government not only finance the recovery of some of the largest
financial institutions in the world, based on the notion that they
are "too big to fail" (which the Lehman Brothers bankruptcy
confirmed), was astonishing in itself. But the American government, via its aid to some of these corporations, became a
major shareholder, demonstrated how far it was prepared to go
in the name of public interest. A very significant lesson can be
drawn from the 2008 financial crisis. A market economy cannot
be left to itself. In a pure and perfectly competitive market in
which production factors are perfectly mobile and all the self-
correction measures kick in at the right time, perhaps the
economy could be left to tick on unsupervised. That model,
however, does not exist, nor has it ever existed. Which won't stop
it from being proposed, since the rich and powerful stand to gain
when government looks the other way and restricts its action to
an efficient education system, low taxes, and absolute minimum
of social legislation.

You can't tell the carpenter by the toolbox

Managing the market economy so as to avoid excess and injustice while maintaining efficiency has always been a complicated operation, or better, set of operations. We are quite familiar with the instruments at our disposal, or the contents of the toolbox, which include regulations of all kinds; aid in the form of grants or fiscal exemptions; refundable or nonrefundable tax credits; straightforward or discriminatory fiscal measures applied to income, transactions or capital; government-owned production or financed corporations, and more. These instruments are known and their impacts have been analysed, but you can't tell the carpenter by the toolbox. Use of these instruments may prejudice certain financial interests. For instance, it has been generally admitted that eliminating the tax on capital will have a beneficial impact on jobs and investment. All other things being equal, that is true in many sectors of production. On the other hand, eliminating taxes on capital for financial institutions has virtually no such positive impact. Governments might decide not to tax to these institutions in the name of fairness or in response to political pressure, but certainly not for reasons of effectiveness.

Knowing how to use the tools in the toolbox is only a starting point; it is also necessary to establish goals, or in other words, to know what works and what does not. From a rational standpoint, as we pointed out at the beginning of this chapter, emphasis should be put on enhancing productivity, and on innovation. That would mean, however, that sectors that are no longer competitive or that are unable to modernize and keep pace would be dropped. Be it the textile, garment, newsprint, softwood lumber, petrochemical, dairy or poultry industries, whatever is doomed to disappear will simply disappear. Government would need only to provide suitable early retirement terms for older workers and facilitate the retraining for younger people, while at the same time focussing most of its energy and resources on its two priorities, productivity and innovation. It is a logical, coherent conclusion, but public opinion would not tolerate a meltdown of such dimensions. Still, the question remains: can we continue to scorn politicians when, as the accusation goes, they throw money out the window in order to get reelected or invest money to keep lame-duck operations in business? The fact is that we are faced with a very delicate exercise that consists in seeking to modify the economy rapidly without touching off a social crisis that might bring the new developments already underway to a halt.

Trading off between provinces

The goal is thus to achieve the right balance, proportions, priorities and intentions, based on how much change society can accept at any given time. This, in fact, is one of the major problems of the Canadian federation. The country is too big and its regions are too disparate and often have conflicting interests. The central government is simply unable to reconcile regional interests, as illustrated by several major issues now before us but also by many others that have marked the country's history.

The federal government, for instance, cannot abandon the automobile industry in Ontario. When the United States government uses all necessary measures to support the recovery of General Motors, Chrysler and, to a lesser extent, Ford, the Canadian government cannot simply refuse to invest the billions of dollars that will keep branch plants in Ontario operating. Inasmuch as Canadian unions agreed to the same sacrifices made by American unions, how could the Canadian government ever stand back and refuse to follow the US lead? The contradiction with what the government is prepared to commit for the forestry and pulp and paper industries, particularly in Quebec, is striking. Here, negligence and obsolescence have slowly destroyed an industry that, from the employment standpoint, is absolutely crucial for certain regions.

In Western Canada, when oil prices are high, Alberta's tar sands represent the second largest oil reserves in the world after Saudi Arabia. Extraction of oil from those tar sands, however, is a massive source of greenhouse gases, and this considerably exacerbates regional disparities in Canada. In tons of annual per capita greenhouse gas emissions (carbon equivalent), Quebec stands at eleven tons, Canada (without Quebec) at twenty-six, with Alberta at seventy-one.[5] Is it surprising that Canada has refused to apply the Kyoto Protocol and constantly dragged its feet leading up to and during the Copenhagen Summit? For many years, Canada's lack of commitment had no concrete impact. The country's reputation for being responsible was sullied, but seen in the light of exemptions granted to China and India for participating in the Kyoto process, the situation did not appear tragic.

A report published in June 2009 by the World Trade Organization and the United Nations Environment Program might well change everything.[6] For the first time, the World Trade Organization has recognized that a country's non-compliance with negotiated environment protection regulations can be considered as discrimination in favour of the country's domestic industries and that, under these conditions, other WTO members can impose carbon taxes aimed at establishing a level playing field. These taxes could be applied to Canadian goods if Canada maintains its current stance, and they would be applied not only to goods from Alberta but to goods from Quebec as well. This could mean additional costs for Quebec of the order of several billions of dollars. This question is discussed further in Chapter 12.

Looking back, we can find many examples of how federal policy has been torn between diverging regional interests. I have witnessed several, but the most egregious was surely the Borden line saga of the mid-1970s. The first oil shock in 1973 quadrupled the price of a barrel of oil. In a move to protect industry in

5. Bloc Québécois, *L'inventaire canadien de gaz à effet de serre*, 1990-2007.
6. WTO and UNEP, *Trade and Climate Change*, Geneva, 2009.

Ontario, the federal government ruled that the price of a barrel of oil in Canada would be lower than the price on the international market. Alberta, which was having difficulty selling its oil to the United States, had no choice but to agree to the federally imposed price, while at the same time it received guarantees that it would have a monopoly on sales of oil and oil products in Ontario. That created a problem: Montreal, where most of the oil in Canada was refined, was purchasing its crude from Venezuela and the Middle East at the international price, while selling some of its refined products in Ontario. The federal government subsidized imported oil to keep the price at the Alberta level, but prohibited the movement of petroleum products from Montreal across a line, known as the Borden line, that was essentially the Ottawa River. Half of Montreal's refineries closed down. Worse yet, Montreal's petrochemical industry, by far Canada's largest, moved to Sarnia, Ontario, and to Edmonton, Alberta. The Quebec government kept some of it alive through Pétromont, a subsidiary of the Société générale de financement, which joined forces with Dow Chemicals to keep an ethylene plant open. Otherwise, the entire industry would have disappeared.[7]

Other confrontations are obviously not as spectacular and, on the industrial front, some joint initiatives taken by the two governments have been very successful. For instance, the Quebec and the federal government joined forces to share the cost of training personnel for the Bell Helicopter plant at Mirabel, north of Montreal. One observation remains nonetheless. It is virtually impossible to develop a coherent and comprehensive industrial policy in which priority is put on productivity and innovation, while keeping certain declining activities alive and allowing others to disappear, but with full support and protection for workers who find themselves unemployed. Environmental protection and land-use planning constraints provide additional challenges.

---

7. Pétromont closed in 2009.

Desperately seeking real government

Focus so far has been on the difficulties encountered in drawing up a coherent set of economic policies. Some details are now in order. The Quebec government and the federal government compete in a wide variety of areas involving support to business, workers and general economic activity. It might have been expected that, as time went by, a form of government "specialization" would have developed and been pursued, but in fact the opposite has occurred. For essentially political reasons, everything has been duplicated. Though efforts to simplify are occasionally made, confusion rapidly rears its ugly head once more. After decades of debate the federal government finally relinquished control over vocational training and allowed Quebec to assume responsibility. But soon thereafter, calls for aid from the federal government were heard, as illustrated in the recent forestry crisis. It should be said however that the desire to achieve an accountant's budgetary balance and maintain a zero deficit is an added incentive for the Quebec government to redirect those who come knocking hat in hand towards benefactors in Ottawa.

In my search for an illustration that would spare the reader a long list of duplications, a very obvious one came to mind. Here is what can be found on the credits page of many books published in Quebec:

> X-Books Publishers gratefully acknowledge the financial support of the Department of Canadian Heritage. We also acknowledge the financial assistance of the Government of Canada through its Canadian Book Publishing Development Program.

> X-Books Publishers also thank the Société de développement des industries culturelles du Québec (SODEC) for its support through through its *Programme de credit d'impôt pour l'édition de livres.*

Each government's claim to represent Quebecers generates competition that can make it difficult—and sometimes impossible—to achieve clear-cut objectives and leads to a proliferation of paperwork. Trying to access government financial support programs is transformed into an obstacle course. With each budget, enterprises must work through page after page of presumed tax breaks and fiscal incentives. The result: a sprinkling of small measures tailored for a handful of specific companies that some day give rise to a battery of complex rules that may or may not meet the needs of these companies. But above all, they demonstrate the sponsoring government's commitment to "promoting economic development."

Government-owned corporations are also obviously part of the prevailing confusion. Recently, for instance, the Caisse de dépôt et placement concluded that investing in small Quebec businesses was a waste of its time. It therefore provided funds to the Business Development Bank of Canada, which in turn finances small Quebec businesses through its Quebec regional offices, now in a position of strength vis à vis the regional offices of Investissement Québec, which offer virtually identical services.

Fortunately, all is not confusion. With regard to tax credits for research and development, the two governments have set aside their rivalry and the program now provides the leverage crucial to the growth of new technologies.

Not everybody complains about competition between governments. It is true that some people have used it to their advantage to advance projects that did not initially generate much excitement. However, it would probably be possible to find a similar number of projects that did not get off the ground because one government used the other government's hesitation to withhold its own support. Indeed, the federal system as practiced causes waste and duplication of efforts. Achieving coherent goals has come to resemble a roll of the dice. From this perspective, an independent Quebec may not be able to guarantee improvement but it will make improvement possible.

Education and economic growth

Before concluding this chapter, I will briefly review the links between education and achievement of our productivity and innovation goals. These questions are closely related: the knowledge economy is more than wishful thinking. Two problems have arisen, one of which only Quebecers themselves can solve, while the other would undoubtedly be easier to settle if the government of Canada kept its distance, but which remains an issue that depends on decisions made in Quebec City. These two problems are first, secondary education and second, university education and research.[8]

Only three of five young Quebecers who begin the seventh grade (Secondary 1 in Quebec) receive their high school leaving diploma (Secondary 5) within five years. The figures for the public school system alone are worse, with the success rate falling to fifty-three percent. And for boys in the Commission scolaire de Montréal, the city's largest French-language school board, the rate drops to thirty-six percent. The English Montreal School Commission in comparison has a success rate of sixty-seven percent, almost twice as high.

Many young people who dropped out return to school after the age of twenty to get their high school diplomas without which they find almost all doors closed to them. Indeed, so many people are trying to make up for lost time that they consume a high percentage of vocational training resources, resulting in shortages for young people in the normal secondary school program.

Similar figures are also carried through to dropout levels at Cegep, Quebec's junior college network; unless rapid remedial action is taken Quebec's future will be at risk. I think we can

---

8. The data on secondary schooling are taken from the *Résultats aux épreuves uniques de juin 2007*, ministère de l'Éducation, 2008. The observations about university education come from my address "Entre l'innovation et le déclin: l'économie québécoise à la croisée des chemins," Les conferences Gérard Parizeau, HEC, 2007.

agree that they represent a tremendous waste in terms of economic growth. Page after page has been, and will be written, on the possible causes and effects. But for our purposes, attention must be focussed on difficulty we face in tying post-secondary professional training to technical training at the Cegep level. As the baby-boom generation reaches retirement age, we are only beginning to realize how poorly the next generation has been prepared. The most striking manifestation is the shortage of technicians in some of Quebec's most dynamic industrial sectors. We must learn how other societies have combined education with internships or apprenticeships. Manual trades also have to be rehabilitated in a world in which technology prevails. Though the workplace has adapted to change, our minds have not kept pace.

Universities are now among the main drivers of economic growth, which represents a departure from the university's traditional vocation Research into the *why's* and *wherefore's* was for a very long time the main issue. Now the question has become *how*. The university's founding vocation still holds in the humanities, social sciences, arts and letters; as a result, Quebec's regional universities play a critical cultural role. Balancing cultural and scientific responsibilities and allocating resources can be a complex task. Academic freedom and the independence of higher education institutions do little to facilitate the development of coherent science policies, particularly during periods of cutbacks and retrenchment. Random intervention by the two levels of government only complicates matters.

We have developed a tendency of reducing everything to dollars and cents, especially when we talk about funding university education. Would two hundred million more be enough? Or is twice that amount required? Will a new campus cost a billion dollars, or can we get by with five hundred million? Government is told that it should not too closely scrutinize how our universities operate. Yet, if we agree that scientific research is the key to innovation and economic growth, then urgently needed additional resources should be earmarked primarily for scientific research, engineering, medicine, biotechnologies, and information technology—those sectors that are the main vectors for innovation and productivity in today's world.

Regional universities

Universities are closely linked to regional economic development. Several of Quebec's regions traditionally depended on exploitation and primary transformation of raw materials. Large corporations were generally the motors of regional development. As productivity improved, private sector employment in these areas declined. For a limited time, the catch-up growth in education and health services provided new public sector employment that masked the loss of employment in the large private companies.

Once public sector growth peaked, these regions were faced with stagnation, and possibly economic decline. One exception to the trend, which also provided new perspectives, was post-secondary teaching and education. Teaching and research in Cegeps and universities became the primary economic growth factor available. The ties between regional universities and businesses provide many examples of local dynamism. Yet it is not clear whether we have learned that lesson or not. Judging by the current regional distribution of Cegep and university funding, it appears not to have sunk in. This comment applies equally to the Canada Foundation for Innovation!

To conclude, in today's wide-open world, where barriers are falling like dominoes and market forces take on overnight an almost universal force, the nation-state has understood that it has only two handles on growth, productivity and innovation. It has also understood that progress and growth cannot emerge from smoking ruins. Democracy cannot tolerate such a thing. Globalization requires rapid change but there are limits to the rate of change that human nature can accommodate. Politics consists of seeking to reconcile these two contradictory forces, exactly that which legitimizes, and strengthens, the role of the state in a globalizing world.

Two governments constantly quarrelling over the same people, both attempting to be the "better" of the two, create dysfunction and waste, but above all an accountability vacuum that leaves the citizen not knowing who is ultimately responsible for what. But the job of government is to govern. That is why they are elected.

Chapter 10

THE STATE AND CORPORATIONS: THE GREAT DEBATE

In the spring of 2009, Quebec's Caisse de dépôt et placement announced massive losses, far higher than what could be explained by the international financial crisis. The chief executive officer of the Caisse had jumped ship. He was replaced and, while people were trying to figure out what had happened, attention turned, both in the Quebec National Assembly and in the media, to closely examine and discuss the mission and operating methods of Quebec's largest financial institution. For a time the head offices of large Quebec corporations came under scrutiny. Some people insisted that it was essential to keep them in Quebec, and that measures had to be taken to make sure they stayed. Financial, industrial and commercial decision-making centres are generators of employment linked to business services, but also to employment in research and development. The Caisse de dépôt et placement had a responsibility in this regard, and while it should not have adopted a "whatever the cost" approach, it should be encouraging efforts to maintain a critical mass of decision-making centres in Quebec.

Leave it to the government...

Others maintained that return on investment was all that counted; if the government wants to maintain that critical decision-making mass, they claim, it simply has to go it alone—but without relying on the Caisse. A statement by the Caisse's then-CEO Henri-Paul Rousseau before the Parliamentary Committee on Public Finance on November 28, 2007 put forward that position succinctly: "There are ways to have industrial policies, to retain prestigious head offices, and to build national champions capable of conquering the planet, but it should not be up to the Caisse to carry out that mission."[1]

At the first press conference held by the Caisse's newly appointed CEO, a reporter asked whether its position would be the same, citing a particular hypothetical case: "If foreign interests attempted to acquire control of Bombardier, would the Caisse try to block them?" The new CEO's answer was hesitant, not to say negative.

Quebec society and business

We now find ourselves at the heart of a fundamental debate, one which has assumed larger proportions in recent years, and is critical for Quebec's future, both, to a certain extent, as a province in Canada, but much more so as an independent society. The debate extends well beyond the problems arising from the relationship between the Quebec government and its leading financial institution, which is unique in North America—and sheds light on the relationship between the government and corporations

Some historical background is required to understand how this came about. French-Canadian society in the mid-twentieth century was incomplete. Talented, hardworking young people could look forward to brilliant careers in the liberal professions, journalism, politics, trade unions, teaching and, of course, in the arts. Business was another story. Quebec society at that time did not hold business careers in the highest regard, but the system

---

1. *Journal des débats*, 35th Legislature, 1st Session, Public Finance Committee, Wednesday, November 28, 2007 (our translation).

was also closed to those who spoke French. After the Conquest, the English, who were backed by Britain's financial might, assumed control when the defeated French departed. For many years, business was almost exclusively the province of the Montreal English-speaking community, with support from London, New York and, later on, Toronto. Obviously, the occasional French-speaking businessman made his mark, but it was an individual accomplishment, certainly not one of a group or a social class.

People of my generation often relate anecdotes to illustrate how hard it was to get ahead in business. The one I best remember occurred when I was representing Lucien Rolland of the Rolland Paper Company on the Trade and Tariffs Committee of the Pulp and Paper Association of Canada. Of the thirty odd members, I was the only one who spoke French. During a meeting in Toronto, we broke for lunch at Toronto's exclusive Granite Club. The treasurer of Dominion Tar and Coal (later to become Domtar) explained how the company had successfully prevented any "Frenchies" from rising above the foreman level at their company's Howard Smith papermaking branch plant, that was located in the Montreal area since the end of the nineteenth century. Suddenly the treasurer saw me listening. Putting his hand to his mouth he said "Oh, sorry Jacques!" Thirty years later the Caisse de dépôt et placement and the Société générale de financement (SGF) took control of Domtar. Some progress has been made.

After World War II, throughout the world, as we noted in a previous chapter, governments intervened to organize social security and to re-launch the economy. In Western Europe, and particularly in France and England, many companies were nationalized; a collectivist economic system was imposed in Eastern Europe. Canada laid emphasis on developing a social safety net, but it also took substantial economic initiatives to finance residential construction, transportation, and support for exports. Even in the United States where nationalization is generally frowned upon, the military-industrial complex had become a powerful motor for economic development.

Fear of communism was strong in Quebec. Under Duplessis, opposition to state interventionism and to trade unions made the Quebec government into a frightened agency that surfed along on post-war prosperity without attempting to change either the economy or social organization. All structuring economic decisions, to use today's jargon, were made outside the French-speaking world. If a pulp and paper plant were to appear at La Tuque on the upper Saint-Maurice River, or a mine in the Abitibi region, or an aluminum smelter in the Saguenay, it meant that a decision had been made somewhere in the vast English-speaking world. French-speakers had very little real influence over the course of events and their future.

During the 1950s, the Quebec economy began to slide. The Toronto Stock Exchange, which took control of financing oil exploration and extraction in the West, displaced the Montreal Stock Exchange. Financial institutions (banks and insurance companies in particular) moved their real head offices to Toronto even though they sometimes maintained an official head office in Montreal to keep up appearances. Construction of the St. Lawrence Seaway prompted industry to move farther west to the other extremity of the Great Lakes. For instance, the decision to transfer the Canadian Car and Foundry works from its location along the Lachine Canal in LaSalle to Thunder Bay on the Northwest shores of Lake Superior cost Quebec thousands of jobs.

Then came the Laurendeau-Dunton report on bilingualism and biculturalism, which included a study on income earned in Quebec. The report clearly established that the French-speaking population had the lowest average income among fourteen ethnic groups with only the Italian-born workers and the Aboriginal population earning less.[2]

---

2. Report of the Royal Commission on Bilingualism and Biculturalism, 1968, Book III, The Work World, p. 23.

Maîtres chez nous (Masters in our own house)

This was the backdrop when the slogan of the Liberal government, first elected in 1960—*Maîtres chez nous*—catapulted Quebec into the Quiet Revolution.[3] The new government adopted simultaneously the principle that René Lévesque had expressed in a single straightforward sentence. "The only tool Quebecers have at their disposal is their government." Whether the term used is "we" or "Quebecers," it was clear that he was referring to the French-speaking population. Semantic gymnastics would have their field day later. The goal was for Quebecers to take responsibility for their own economic development. Looking back, it is often thought that the Quebec model, or Québec Inc. as it is sometimes referred to, had been planned. Not so; there was never a comprehensive plan. There were however some basic principles. The first consisted in correcting the ways that markets operated and prevented or retarded industrial development. This in turn led to the creation of government-owned corporations such as Sidbec, SOQUEM, SOQUIP, and to the acquisition of two asbestos producers. There was nothing dogmatic about these initiatives. If there was a problem, there had to be a solution. The results ranged from excellent, to nil and very expensive. Nationalization of the private electricity utilities obviously constituted a special case that led to the development of a fundamental pillar of the Quebec economy.

An inalienable financial system

The second principle concerned the establishment of a real Quebec financial system adapted to Quebec's financial needs and able to compete with Canadian and foreign financial institutions operating in Quebec. These Quebec institutions would preferably be sheltered from takeover by external interests.

---

3. *Maître chez nous* or Masters in Our Own House became the campaign slogan for the 1962 general election.

Until recently, that aim could have been considered accomplished. There is no simple explanation. But, it is a fact that Quebec society, which for generations had been unable to devise ways to finance and carry out its collective projects, became remarkably self-sufficient in financial terms.

Fully half of Quebec's individual savings were deposited in cooperatives belonging to the Mouvement Desjardins. The most popular commercial bank for Quebec's small and medium-sized businesses, the National Bank of Canada, operated mainly in Quebec and, until recently, no single shareholder could hold more than ten percent of the bank's shares. The largest life insurance company, Industrielle Alliance, was a mutual company. When it decided to become a joint stock corporation, it persuaded the Quebec National Assembly to include in its charter a clause to the effect that no shareholder could hold more than ten percent of the shares. The Fonds de solidarité FTQ, which holds Quebec's largest reserves of venture capital, belongs to Quebec's largest trade union federation. Investissement Québec, the Société générale de financement and the Caisse de dépôt et placement are government-owned corporations or agencies. Until recently, Montreal had its own stock exchange, a useful instrument for issuing shares that include specific Quebec fiscal advantages. The ten-percent rule also applied to the Montreal Stock Exchange. In a nutshell, Quebec's financial system was inalienable.

Such a financial system corresponds to the needs of an independent country. The only thing missing is a link with the central bank, currently the Bank of Canada, through a clearing agency. It is quite remarkable that all this came into being without the question of Quebec's future being explicitly raised. Paradoxically this "system"—the accurate term since it was devised as a system—was never perceived as such.

Cracks have begun to appear, however, and some of its original components have been abandoned. The first breach occurred when the federal government amended the Bank Act boosting the ceiling level for shares in a chartered bank held by a single shareholder to twenty percent. A single shareholder, however, was allowed to own all the shares in two small banks, and another category of bank was created for those in which shareholder equity was between one and five billion dollars. In this case, a single shareholder could acquire sixty-five percent of shares on the condition that the other shares were widely distributed among a large number of shareholders. Only one bank in Canada fit into this category: the National Bank of Canada. The bank's senior managers, who at that time held a large quantity of stock-options, requested the change and the federal government readily agreed. In the end, control of the bank was not sold because of resistance from a group of members of the board of directors (and because of the significant upswing in the value of the bank's share). The Caisse de dépôt et placement adopted a very curious attitude during the episode. The Caisse owns shares in some sixty banks around the world. In Canada, it held a major share in TD Bank; at the end of 2007, it held more than a billion dollars worth of shares in Power Corporation and its subsidiaries; it responded favourably to CIBC's request when that bank wanted to increase its capital. Yet the Caisse owns no National Bank shares, which clearly indicates that it would not oppose an attempt to buy control of the main source of commercial credit for Quebec's small and medium-sized businesses. At about the same time that the federal Bank Act was being amended the Montreal Stock Exchange, which belonged to Montreal brokers and financial institutions, was selling all its conventional stock exchange operations to the Toronto Stock Exchange, keeping only derivative operations under an agreement with Toronto.[4] So successful was the new formula that the new owners decided to sell these operations to Toronto as well.

---

4. The decision was made on March 15, 1999 and the transfer was effective on December 3, 1999. The ten-percent provision was in force until then. It was abolished.

Quebec's regulatory body, the Autorité des marchés financiers, obtained certain guarantees that operations would remain in Montreal. However, the federal government's decision to establish a federal securities commission might simply bring all stock exchange activity in Montreal to an end.[5]

Supporting the *garde montante* (the rising generation)

The third principle underlying the relationship between government and business was the government's responsibility to provide all the support it could to the development of a French-speaking business class capable of assuming, and in fact assuming, the key decision-making in companies Quebec society relies upon to ensure its prosperity. That is what I once described in a budget speech as the *garde montante* or the rising generation. There is nothing partisan about this notion. Both Liberal and Parti Québécois governments have systematically worked towards the same goal. The ways and objectives were clearly defined over a long period. In recent years, however, confusion has set in, first because the rules of interprovincial and international trade have changed, but also because the spread of neo-liberal ideas has given rise to a pervasive distrust of big government and what are assumed to be its evils. Most of the groundwork had been laid, however, and the rising generation had solidly taken root. Now and in the future, the challenge is to see Quebec businesses thrive in a North American and world context, rather than only within the Canadian context.

The first step was the nationalization of the private electricity utilities, something achieved in Ontario in 1906. Hydro-Québec was faced with enormous construction programs that took on even greater proportions when hydropower development in the James Bay area was launched. Hydro-Québec became a dis-

---

5. Many countries with populations smaller than, or similar to Quebec's have maintained their own stock exchanges.

tributor of contracts far beyond anything that Quebec had ever experienced. Its purchasing power was extraordinary.

Hydro-Québec's policy was based on three fundamental elements. The first consisted in systematically turning to Quebec-based engineering firms. Consulting engineering firms like SNC (Surveyer, Nenniger et Chênevert) and Lavalin quickly joined the major leagues in consulting engineering in North America. The second element consisted in establishing, in all public bidding, a ten-percent preferential rating for Quebec-made products over those from elsewhere in Canada, with a further ten-percent applied to foreign products. Ratings were adjusted according to the percentage of Quebec content. The third element consisted in providing guarantees of major multi-year procurement orders to foreign companies that agreed to establish facilities in Quebec. Nor can we neglect Hydro-Québec's role in developing the use of French in technical operations, which until then were entirely conducted in English.

The Société de développement industriel (SDI), forerunner to Investissement Québec, drew up strict criteria regulating the support it was authorized to provide to companies. Support would only be forthcoming if all the services used (e.g., accounting, legal, computer support, consulting engineering) were provided by Quebec companies.

The goal of the Quebec Stock Saving Plan (Régime d'Épargne-Actions) was likewise threefold. The first aim was to prompt Quebecers to acquire shares in companies, where they lagged far behind the rest of North America. The second aim to allow people in high income tax brackets to pay less on the condition that they participated in the Plan. The third aim was to provide access to venture capital for Quebec companies in response to complaints that it was not available. Shares eligible for the plan had to be issued by companies whose head office or primary place of business were in Quebec. In the beginning, people could deduct a dollar from their taxable income for each dollar spent on the stock saving plan shares. People obviously bought shares in Bell, the Royal Bank or the National Bank, and gradually became accustomed to doing so. The fiscal benefits were then reduced for shares in the very large companies, but were increased for small and medium-size businesses. That opened the door to companies like Cascades, Bombardier, Jean Coutu, Couche-Tard, CGI, and so forth.

The Fonds de solidarité FTQ was created at the initiative of the late Louis Laberge, President of Quebec's labour federation, the Fédération des travailleurs et des travailleuses du Québec, and Fernand Daoust, its Secretary General, to support or create jobs in Quebec companies. The Fonds de solidarité had a revolutionary impact owing to both the extent of involvement it engendered among workers and its mere size. The tax benefits granted by the Quebec government led to such massive investment of funds that the government—a Liberal government at that time—fixed a ceiling on the funds collected annually. The following government (Parti Québécois) agreed to raise that ceiling but only on condition that more capital would be made available for the regional solidarity funds that had also been created.

A federalist government (Jean Lesage) drew up Hydro-Quebec's procurement policy. Another federalist government (Robert Bourassa) adopted the operating rules of the Société de développement industriel. A sovereigntist government (René Lévesque) established the Quebec Stock Saving Plan and supported the creation of the Fonds de solidarité FTQ.

A common thread ran through all these initiatives: they were designed to foster the creation and development of Quebec companies and to familiarize Quebecers with the workings of business and companies so that they would come to see it as an integral part of Quebec society and essential tools for economic growth and employment.

It is no longer possible to establish programs so systematically discriminatory as Hydro-Québec's procurement policy. Both in Canada and in dealings with other countries, such explicit methods of operation are not allowed. But it is no longer necessary to go so far. Most investment decisions in Quebec are now made by Quebec businesses. Quebecers often head Quebec-based subsidiaries of foreign-owned corporations. Continued efforts are made by Quebec to induce foreign corporations to invest in Quebec, as is the case elsewhere in the world. Quebec is no longer dependent on decisions made everywhere else but Quebec. Above all, there is no lack of capital. During crises, capital can be more cautious and even skittish, but overall, Quebec society has become a society like any other.

The problems it faces are the same ones that confront all industrialized societies today. But though the questions are similar, countries can respond in a variety of ways.

The first question is that of privatization, a global trend. For many years, private companies were nationalized because no other way was seen to bring about the changes that had to be made. Hydro-Québec was a case in point. Nationalization represented the only way to set up an integrated power generation, transmission and distribution system with uniform electricity rates throughout Quebec. Other examples have been mentioned, such as Sidbec and Asbestos Corporation. In general, however, the Quebec government put less emphasis on nationalization than on the creation of government-owned corporations that, in turn, acquired private companies (e.g., the Société générale de financement (SGF)). But in all cases, the question remains: whether or not to privatize, and when and how it should be done?

By far the most intriguing case is that of Hydro-Québec, the locomotive of Quebec's economic success. The transformations that it was established to bring about were successful in every respect. But Hydro-Québec no longer has any revolutions to lead, but it must be managed optimally in the interest of all Quebecers. It is profitable, with net profits year after year representing about twenty percent of its annual sales figures. When the Quebec government decided to consolidate Hydro-Québec revenues with those of the government, it placed itself in a glaring conflict of interest since the government's budgetary balance sheet improves with every electricity rate increase. Rates are, however, controlled by a regulatory agency, the Régie de l'électricité et du gaz, that attempts to assuage the finance minister's appetite.

Hydro-Québec could be privatized in several ways. Based on different examples in the world, three main models appear feasible. The first consists in selling a substantial portion of the share capital that would remain a minority of total capital. A dividend policy would be established with the aim of distributing shares among many portfolios that could be considered as a "reasonable person's" investment. The government would remain the majority shareholder and ensure that the utility is managed with a long-term perspective with a priority to research and development.

Under the second formula, the government would accept a minority shareholder position. Private interests, not necessarily Quebecers, would be responsible for managing Hydro-Québec, but the government would continue to hold enough shares to make its presence felt on the board of directors and could possibly rely on the Caisse de dépôt et placement to increase its influence, depending however on the state of mind of those responsible for managing the Caisse. Pressure to radically raise rates could become critical in light of the enormous amounts of money at play.

The third formula consists in gradually selling off all the shares with the government keeping only a single share known as the *Golden Share*, which would prevail over all other shares as regards decisions provided by law, i.e., transfer abroad of control of the corporation or of its head office to or major changes in its operations.

This formula, invented by the Thatcher government in the United Kingdom, was later adopted by several other countries, mainly in Europe. Recently, when Brazil's Vale Corporation sought to acquire International Nickel, the Canadian company that was the world's largest nickel producer at the time, people realized that a *Golden Share* protected the Brazilian company, while International Nickel was unprotected. Vale ended up acquiring International Nickel in 2006.

As things stand now, Hydro-Québec is very valuable. If electricity rates were boosted to the level of Ontario's rates, as many members of Quebec's elite demand, the complete sale of Hydro-Québec would entirely eliminate Quebec's debt.[6]

Obstacles: income taxes and the public

These proposals, that deserve to be discussed, cannot be carried very far in the current federal context. A fundamental principle underlying our political system is that the state cannot tax the state. In this case, the federal government cannot tax a provincially owned corporation. From a fiscal standpoint, a government-owned corporation is defined as a company or an agency in which the government owns at least ninety percent of the shares. This means that only ten percent of Hydro-Québec's shares could be privatized. In order to envisage any of the formulas outlined above, we are faced with two choices. Either Hydro-Québec would no longer be a government-owned corporation, which means that its profits would be taxed at the same rate as any other large Canadian company (nineteen percent of its profits would go to Ottawa), or Quebec would have to become an independent country.

Attention must also be paid to the tax burden. When a government that holds a very profitable monopoly decides to increase rates, it is in fact levying a tax. There are no two ways about it. It is completely nonsensical for Quebec to constantly align itself with Ontario whenever prices, income taxes or other taxes in Quebec are lower than Ontario's, without lowering the prices,

---

6. Jean-François Lisée explains this question very clearly in his book *Pour une gauche efficace*, Montreal, Boréal, 2008, pp. 76-77. In his opinion, rate increases would be compensated through lowered income taxes.

income taxes or other taxes that are higher than Ontario's. Yes, Quebec income taxes are higher than in Ontario, and electricity rates are lower. It is probably just fine that way as long as Quebec has enough electricity to satisfy its export requirements.[7]

In the final analysis, public reaction must be taken into consideration. For a great many Quebecers of a certain age, Hydro-Québec is the symbol of Quebec's collective success and a source of pride and achievement. Hydro-Québec put an end to a collective inferiority complex. It was done cleanly, above board and with no scandals, and in French to boot. It is a government-owned utility and national institution that must be handled with care! Twice in the past, I suggested that Hydro-Québec sell off ten percent of its shares so as to open the door to public financial participation in what is Quebec's finest asset. Both times the suggestion was met with an immediate negative reaction. People like their Hydro-Québec as it is. The old slogan *"Nous sommes tous Hydro-Québécois"* (We are all Hydro-Quebecers) has solid roots.

To sum up: Quebec possesses an extremely valuable asset. Any assessment of Quebec assets and debt that fails to take Hydro-Québec into account, as is often the case, is necessarily flawed.

The importance of decision-making centres

Our analysis has now brought us back to our starting point, namely decision-making centres. In Quebec, this question cannot be discussed without reference to the Caisse de dépôt et placement, which is at the core of any such policy. There are no two ways about it; we are talking about wielding economic power. Those who debate or cross swords on this issue know perfectly

---

7. In the case of shortages, energy savings must be considered as an option. Neither as finance minister nor as premier was I ever able to establish which had a higher marginal cost, a kilowatt-hour saved or a kilowatt-hour generated. These complicated questions require more thought than simply saying that the consumer will pay.

well that it is not a question of approving or opposing a market economy. We all recognize the same rules. But the question is: where will decisions be made and who will make them? The statement made by former Caisse CEO Henri-Paul Rousseau, referred to at the beginning of this chapter, could not have been clearer. Quebec may well want to have its leaders and industrial champions, but it is not the Caisse's business; it is up to the government. Since the government is neither equipped nor organized to handle the job by itself and since the institution that should be its number one partner is nowhere to be seen, nothing happens. In today's global economy, it is irresponsible to sit back and look on as the merger and acquisition movement hits the country's largest companies. The argument on return on investment—legislation on the Caisse uses the term "optimal" as if it had the slightest operational meaning—is the bludgeon used to terminate any discussion in favour of government intervention in corporate strategies. How much easier it is to take in money freely, then invest it in financial operations, than to partner with entrepreneurs. A flagrant opposition has now been created between finance-based and entrepreneurial economics. It is easier to speculate than to create employment and participate in innovation. Moreover, the return is often superior... that is until the next meltdown, as in 2008. After such enormous losses, it is time to stop repeating that pensions are better protected through financial operations than through investment in industrial and commercial operations and in services. It was the financial crisis that provoked the economic crisis, and not the other way around.

The responsibility of the Caisse de dépôt et placement

The Caisse's primary responsibility is to Quebec, where all its funds come from. Moreover, given the magnitude of the funds it manages, the Caisse is also a major player in the Quebec economy. It holds Quebec's largest public sector investment portfolio, it has the largest real estate portfolio and the largest portfolio of company shares. It cannot be a Pontius Pilate, and, by the same token, the government cannot claim that it does not know what's going on at the Caisse.

From its inception in 1965 until 1981, the Caisse invested only in Quebec and in Canada according to strict guidelines and based on the cautionary principles that guide life insurance companies. Shares in corporations that the Caisse could acquire were defined in Section 981(o) of the Civil Code as the investment of a responsible person. A basket clause limited the maximum value of investments the Caisse could hold that did not comply with regulatory provisions at seven percent of total assets. Even under these restrictions, the capacity of the Caisse to acquire shares in corporations encountered considerable opposition from those opposed to the government involvement in the operations of corporations. At the end of this period the idea surfaced that the Caisse had become too big and that it had to be divided up into pieces, which would be a way of diluting the government's influence. The size of the Caisse did in fact begin to raise certain problems, particularly with respect to stocks and bonds, since the Caisse was seen as having an excessive influence on markets.

As Quebec finance minister, I authorized the Caisse to begin purchasing stocks and acquiring participations in other countries. For several years, equity participations were often linked to the Quebec economy. For instance, the Caisse acquired interest in the capital of an American aluminum company at a time when it was expanding its Quebec facilities.

Financial institutions were then deregulated; the Quebec government joined the movement enthusiastically, as far as the Caisse was concerned. Then came the 2004 Act under which the Caisse was allowed to participate in the latest and most exotic transactions in which the lost control of the rules of application. The Caisse could basically do whatever it wanted. It then became one of the world's largest sovereign funds. The largest of these had assets valued at nine hundred billion dollars. Another small group had between four hundred and six hundred billion, and another dozen had between two hundred and four hundred billion. With its two hundred and sixty billion dollars in assets, the Caisse was in the major leagues.[8] It became the number two shareholder of the world's largest airport management firm, and the largest real estate investor in France (ahead of the Arab sheiks). It borrowed the equivalent of half of the assets of its depositors so as to enter into a variety of exciting financial transaction. Quebec was no longer the main objective. The Caisse's global calling was supposed to produce remarkable returns and all Quebec pensioners had to do was sit back and applaud. In Quebec, it invested as though Quebec were a mature market in which funds were invested indiscriminately but with no specific responsibility.

Such was the globalized vision that has now fallen apart. Temporarily perhaps. For a year or two, things will proceed calmly, profits will be declared, until the time comes to go global once again.

It is as plain as day that an independent Quebec cannot allow the Caisse to define its own orientations. It is simply too dangerous. In the days following a successful referendum, there will be considerable turbulence and the Caisse, along with other institutions, will be called upon to set aside a significant amount of liquid assets.[9] That alone would have a calming effect on markets. The next steps are well known, just as it is known that, in this area, the Caisse cannot lose. But what if the Caisse stayed inactive? And what if it announced that it would leave it up to market forces to decide? And, to be ironic, that it was more interested in investing in China?

Once Quebec has become an independent country, once it is understood that the Canadian dollar is also the currency of the new country, and that the NAFTA zone or free trade with the

---

8. Total assets to December 31, 3007.
9. The O Plan of 1995.

United States will be maintained, it would be necessary to define the role of the new country's largest institution in terms of accumulated capital, on the same footing in terms of assets as the Desjardins Mouvement and the National Bank.

The Caisse de dépôt et placement in an independent Quebec

Once the government has been changed, its most urgent task will be to restore the elementary, prudential rules of operation. The Caisse is not a hedge fund and should not be taking the same risks as those who gamble with their own money. This means that investment rules must be revised, and that certain types of unhedged transactions, derivative operations and abusive and dangerous recourse to leverage must be prohibited. The government must approve investment rules. Some will decry government interference in the independence of the Caisse. Exactly. The government will be interfering. Nobody has the right to manipulate a large portion of the savings of the citizens of a country without surveillance and without having to report fully once a year. The experiment has been made and it failed! Time has come to return to a more reasonable approach.

The next step will be to define the tasks of the Caisse in Quebec and in other countries. It would be absurd, but also impossible, to force the Caisse to invest all its funds in Quebec. Rules must be established for the Caisse in Quebec (which would also extend to Canada inasmuch as companies in these two countries remain integrated as they are now) and other rules for its activities in other countries. These rules will not be the same because the Caisse, as we have said, has different responsibilities towards Quebec from those it has toward other countries.

In Quebec, the Caisse should facilitate public debt management, like a central bank in most countries. This would involve technical operations, the strategy for which is established by the finance ministry that designates the financial institution that will perform them. These operations do not involve risk, and certainly nothing comparable to the risk involved in the Asset Backed Commercial Paper (ABCP) that the Caisse created and then attempted to manage.

The Caisse does not have to act like a Quebec entrepreneur. It should support entrepreneurs, finance them, drop them when necessary, and participate in merger and acquisition operations, without government authorization or disapproval. But it must understand the policies developed by the government and help bring them to fruition insofar as these policies seem to be compatible with its own interests. The exercise is a delicate, difficult and complicated one, which can only be properly achieved if the Caisse's CEO can enjoy the ironclad protection that only the Quebec National Assembly as a whole can provide. The provisions of the original Act respecting the Caisse must be restored so the CEO can be replaced only after a vote in the National Assembly. Once that has been done, the finance minister can clearly express his or her disagreement with a CEO who does not wish to insist, for instance, that control of Bombardier remains in Quebec. Henri-Paul Rousseau's statement, quoted at the beginning of this chapter, would make no sense in an independent Quebec.

This does not mean that every sale of a large Quebec company to foreign interests should be blocked. It would be illogical to seek control of companies in the United States while prohibiting the opposite from occurring here.

Nor does it mean in any way that return on investment is not a priority. However, seeking that return must not involve taking enormous financial risk and low entrepreneurial risk. We know what that can cause. It is time to return to the rules of common sense such as diversification, minority participations that help understand what is happening and make it possible to influence decision-making, and a certain sense of proportion. For instance, there is no sense in boasting about losing one hundred million dollars in a large Quebec-controlled multinational and two billion dollars in a London airport management firm.

Once a clear idea has been established as to the Caisse's role and responsibilities in Quebec and for the rest of the world, the best return possible should be sought, but a return that is compatible with the risks appropriate for an institution that manages pensions. Still, it could be very attractive to help a Quebec multinational that wishes to acquire a subsidiary or a distribution network in the United States, Europe or China... Nothing is simple. Public interest is not always easy to interpret, but it must always prevail over all others.

Chapter 11

THE STATE AND THE CITIZEN (PART 1)

The previous chapter dealt with the relationship between the state and business—a relationship that is the key to economic growth and prosperity. This chapter will take up the relationship between the state and its citizens, which is where the impact of all economic, financial and social programs is felt. Some societies are prosperous or even rich according to the statistics, but they are headed by royal families and have poor populations with no future. Other societies are booming, but the air they breathe is totally polluted and the streets are dangerous. The ultimate goal of economic development is to achieve prosperity, share it fairly among the people, and ensure equal opportunity and a satisfactory life style for all.

In Quebec, to varying degrees, these three goals have been substantially attained. René Lévesque often said Quebec's political situation was by no means a gulag. Still, Quebecers are faced with a number of problems, some of them serious, others less so, which have lasted too long and, for political reasons, do not seem to get solved. As we have repeatedly demonstrated in these pages, certain issues fail to be resolved not only from one year to the next, but from one generation to the next. The consequences of these failures may differ, but taken as a whole, they suggest a stultified society that is no longer capable of moving forward. But we must not oversimplify the search for solutions. Quebec independence is not a miracle cure; it will not automatically make

Quebecers more intelligent. But it will not make them dumber either. Policy and program choices and political will—perhaps political will above all else—can help speed change. It should not be forgotten, however, that today's problems sometimes stem from the shortcomings of those who hold power or who have held it in the past. On another level, some questions—environmental issues automatically spring to mind—can only be solved globally and results will only be achieved when the most populated countries reach agreement. This does not mean that Quebecers have no role to play. Furthermore, certain problems can only be solved satisfactorily when Quebec becomes an independent country.

Training, taxation, language and environment

I will avoid attempting to cover too much ground. My belief is that it is better to have clear ideas on a small number of questions than to produce long lists of ideas. It is vital to understand how to address a few of the real problems that affect day-to-day life. The following four issues are fundamental and encompass many others:

1. Vocational and technical training, adapting to the market and unemployment protection;
2. Distribution of revenue and taxation;
3. The French language: how to ensure that Quebec lives and works in French;
4. The environment: what Quebecers should and can do to counter climate change.

The first refers to a condition that is essential for economic growth and people's incomes. What must be done to substantially increase income, limit unemployment, and ensure that each generation enjoys a better life than the previous one?

The second issue is twofold: are Quebecers taxed too heavily or badly taxed? Is wealth properly distributed? How can we ensure that everybody assumes their share of the fiscal burden and that tax loopholes are plugged? Decisions are made based on a certain concept of social justice; they also have a substantial impact on the way the economy develops. How can a proper balance be achieved?

The question of the French language is a complex one. For people of my generation, French has made tremendous strides because of the French Language Charter or Bill 101. But has French effectively become the language of work in Quebec? English-language schools do not properly prepare students to earn their living in French, while French-language schools do not prepare students well enough for life in North America. Ottawa imposes bilingualism, yet for Quebec French is the official language. How are immigrants to integrate, and into what society?

The fourth question has become very dear to Quebecers: protection of the environment and, more specifically, climate change. Considering the reticence in the United States and Canada, can environment policy be anything other than a Quebec issue? Does the carbon exchange have a future?

I am fully aware that all of these questions are multifaceted, but answers must be found. Moreover, it is important to determine what can be solved in the current political system and what will require a change of political systems.

It is widely known now that among the conditions that enable companies to remain dynamic and competitive, two specifically concern the workforce. The first is the capacity to hire and lay-off employees with a certain amount of flexibility. The second is its access to a well-trained workforce.

Workforce flexibility and worker protection

Workforce flexibility is not as simple as it may appear. If employees can be laid off without solid financial protection or if the right to fire employees becomes an expression of unbridled capitalism, the state will intervene sooner or later and severely regulate corporations. In order to maintain as much employment flexibility as possible, it is necessary to establish not only a generous unemployment insurance system, but also a way to ensure that once the unemployment benefits have been exhausted the unemployed do not fall into a poverty trap from which it can be difficult to escape.

The second condition concerns manpower training, which must be provided before a young person enters the workforce and be available throughout his or her career. Companies cannot expect to have full flexibility to hire and lay off employees, and at the same time refuse all responsibility for training the workforce. Government has every right to demand (with appropriate incentives) that increased protection of earnings go hand in hand with continued job training. In Quebec, and in Canada, people have had a hard time grasping these principles, and each level of government has worked towards different objectives.

In order to eliminate the huge deficits that, at one point, were equal to half of budgetary revenues, Ottawa began to use unemployment insurance as leverage to solve the problem. By drastically reducing both accessibility to unemployment insurance and the benefits available and by maintaining contributions well above what this so-called insurance could justify, the federal government transformed the program—renaming it employment insurance—into a form of theft. It is easier now to understand how the federal government balanced its budget and also how it accumulated such large surpluses during the ten years before the 2008-09 recession. When the recession began, half of the unemployed were ineligible for employment insurance!

Quebec controls last-resort assistance in the form of welfare. Efforts were made over some fifteen years to limit access to welfare, but above all the base rates were kept at deliberately low levels, while incentives were created to encourage welfare recipients to register in training programs and reintegrate the workforce. In 1996-97, average annual welfare payments (in inflation-adjusted dollars to 2005) were 8,819 dollars compared to 7,873 in 2005-06.

For many years, both governments have experimented with vocational training and reintegration. The Canada-United States Free Trade Treaty, for example, contains detailed provisions, which have rarely been used. In Quebec, experiments were initiated as early as 1982, even during the recession.

Ottawa's vocational training programs were transferred to Quebec in 1998. Quebec imposed a tax of one percent of total payroll in 1995 for training purposes, but companies could obtain exemptions if they provided their own training for their personnel. That system, however, was recently dismantled.

Dysfunction and waste

The high school and junior college system is organized to provide vocational and technical training for both young people and adults, however, as we noted earlier, dropout and failure rates have remained high. The social and economic cost of maintaining such high dropout and low education rates is substantial. Economist Pierre Fortin illustrated the point with the following figures. The chart below shows the employment rates and average weekly salaries of workers between twenty-five and fifty-four years old in 2007, by level of education attained.[1]

	Employment rate	Weekly salary
No high school diploma	61%	$573
Secondary school leaving	78%	$682
Vocational or Cegep certificate	86%	$743
University degree	88%	$1,004

In addition to being very stingy, the Canadian and Quebec system—if we dare use the word—is a model of incoherence and inefficiency. Employers in Canada and Quebec have typical

---

1. Quoted in Luc Godbout and Suzie St-Cerny, *Le Québec, un paradis pour les familles*, Québec, Presses de l'Université Laval, p. 37.

North American freedom to fire or lay off and have even fewer obligations than in the United States. In that country, unemployment insurance is linked to an experience rating system that penalizes employers that regularly lay off employees and rewards those that lay off less frequently. What the Americans provide is minimal compared to protection in Europe. Not only do such systems not even exist in Canada: the exact opposite holds true: Workers who change jobs too often are penalized.

The unemployed are only partially insured, in a limited manner, and for only a short time, but in order to be eligible for welfare, they must show that they are almost destitute. Cautious people who save get incentives to contract debts or sell off everything they own.[2]

Vocational training

The employer is not systematically expected to cooperate in worker training (other than on an ad hoc basis). When a recession sets in and unemployment rises rapidly (forty-eight percent increase between July 2008 and July 2009 in Ontario, twenty-three percent in Quebec), people are left to get by as best they can. Occasionally when the situation is particularly severe (e.g., the forestry crisis), public pressure forces the governments to create special programs for older workers, for example, but these programs lack any overarching vision or perspective. Quite significantly, in the middle of the 2009 recession the government and the Official Opposition in Ottawa decided to strike a committee to study possible employment insurance amendments that would enable the minority government to survive. At the same time, the Council of the Federation, which includes the provinces and territories, studied the same question and remained unmoved and deafeningly silent on the Quebec premier's proposal to find ways to link employment insurance

---

2. Jean-François Lisée, *Pour une gauche efficace, op. cit.*, p. 147. Several factual elements in this chapter are based on Jean-François Lisée's book.

reform with vocational training. A similar reaction took place when the OECD proposed in 2004 that Canada either adopt the American experience rating policy or establish specific ratings based on experience.

The "system" is in fact unfair, inefficient and, quite frankly, dishonest. In the interest of the productivity of Quebec businesses, as well as in the name of worker protection and enhanced living standards, this system—which is really not a system—should not be modified but created from scratch. Only a single government can achieve this. Too many countries have been successful (Scandinavia, for example, or even the United Kingdom and Germany) for people to continue trying to convince themselves that disorder of this magnitude is inevitable.

Minimal requirements

It would take more than a few pages to describe how a coherent Quebec system might work, but we do know that such a system should consist of several basic elements.

1. Young people must have access to a real vocational and technical option. The program must include internships with companies. The option must lead to a diploma. Incentives to ensure completion of vocational education should be considered.

2. Adult workers must have the right to obtain training, either on the job or elsewhere, whether to upgrade skills or change trades. In recent years, many countries have recognized this right and have acted to enable workers to actually take advantage of it. The British *skills account* is a remarkable innovation. Since its launch in 2001, nearly four million people have opened "their account" and fifty thousand companies are participating.[3]

---

3. "Every person in Great Britain who is interested can have a skills account making it possible to establish the level of training, financial aid, direct support (e.g., daycare and transportation for single parents) required in order to learn or relearn to read and to get past the technical level and reach the

3. Unemployment should lead quickly to assistance in finding employment and improving skills in the person's current area of work or in preparation for a career change.

4. Last-resort assistance for employable people should not be unconditional. It should include requirements, but also provide for a decent standard of living.

This would be a major shift, one that would set up a new layer of administration. Businesses will be solicited more than ever before, but participation would be very much in their interest. For trade unions, it would undoubtedly be a challenge unlike any they have faced before. The project would be of a similar magnitude to Quebec's Quiet Revolution in education in the 1960s. Now as then, the government must assume full charge.

Taxes and redistribution

Although Canada's federal system has proven a serious obstacle to the formulation of efficient employment and manpower training policies, the same cannot be said about individual income taxation and redistribution of revenue. Since 1972, when the provinces were able to set their own fiscal policies in those areas permitted by the Canadian Constitution, successive Quebec governments have set goals and come to realize that they have the means to achieve those goals. Two examples illustrate this point: the fight against poverty and, more importantly, family policy.

Two questions cannot, however, be addressed within the current political system: control of provincial taxes levied on corporate profits and tax evasion through the use of offshore tax havens has proven to be very difficult. We will return to these questions shortly.

It has become a commonplace to say that Quebec's income tax is higher than anywhere in North America. True enough, if

professional level." Jean-François Lisée, *Pour une gauche efficace, op. cit.,* p. 145.

we look at tax rates. However, when we factor in social contributions (i.e., contributions to the Quebec pension plan, the RRQ) as well as benefits provided to individuals through Quebec fiscal policy (i.e., tax credits of various kinds), or, in other words, when net fiscal burden for different categories of taxpayers with different incomes is included in the mix, the picture is quite different.[4]

Quebec is not fiscal hell

Studies conducted by Professor Luc Godbout have helped to dissipate alarmist statements about Quebec fiscal policy. The conclusion of his most recent study is particularly enlightening and deserves to be quoted in its entirety.

Results for fiscal 2008, which avoid the trap of comparing the fiscal burden based only on income taxes, provide an interesting picture of the fiscal burden in Quebec and its recent evolution.

Overall, it does not appear to be greater than elsewhere. Even though Quebec levies higher income taxes than other G7 countries, lower social contributions demanded combined with generous benefits resulting from fiscal policy mean that Quebec's results compare favourably with those of other G7 countries.

· It follows that Quebec's net fiscal burden for 2008 is never higher than the other G7 countries.
· Quite the opposite in, fact; Quebec's net fiscal burden for all cases presented falls consistently below G7 and OECD averages.
· Furthermore, when the results of fiscal 2008 and 2000 are compared, Quebec emerges as a tax reduction leader.
· In all cases, Quebec achieved the greatest reductions in net fiscal burden as expressed by percentage points between 2000 and 2008.
· In a classification of G7 countries, Quebec had either improved its relative position in 2008 or remained in the lead.

---

4. A single person, a couple with no children, a single parent with children. For income, fractions or multiples of average salaries are used.

· While this was being accomplished, a more specific comparison with the United States shows significant improvement in the competitive position of Quebec's fiscal burden. While in 2000, Quebec and the United States were on an equal footing, with half of the analysed cases putting Quebec in a favourable position, and the other half, the United States. In 2008, Quebec was in a favourable position in six of the eight cases analysed. And in the two cases in which Quebec lagged behind, it had reduced the gap from about five percentage points to less than one percentage point.

The present research report, thanks to the approach developed by the OECD, demonstrates the importance of accurately comparing fiscal burdens and allows us to dismiss the erroneous notion that Quebec is a so-called fiscal hell.[5]

That, in my opinion, settles the matter. The income tax structure is by no means perfect, however. It is clear, for example, that the maximum tax rate is reached much too soon, at about $80,000. Increases leading up to that point are too steep and the burden is too great on average incomes, whereas those with higher incomes get off too easily. The rate is the same for incomes of $80,000 and $300,000. Making corrections will be expensive and can only be done gradually with the use of other sources of taxation. This of course refers to transaction taxes, known as value-added taxes (VAT) in many countries and as the goods and services tax (GST) in Canada, which is to a certain extent harmonized with provincial sales taxes (the TVQ in Quebec).

That most countries use the value-added tax should come as no surprise. Consumers pay the tax, which represents no burden for businesses. It does not drive down prices on export goods but it is paid on consumer-purchased imported goods. In short, exports are not hindered and imports are taxed just like domestic

---

5. Luc Godbout and Suzie St-Cerny, *Année d'imposition 2008: la charge fiscale nette des particuliers au Québec et dans le G7. La palme au Québec, est-ce possible?* Sherbrooke, Université de Sherbrooke, Chaire de recherche en fiscalité et finances publiques, pp. 22-23.

goods. There can be a single rate, or a number of rates. It can be applied on everything or certain goods considered to be essential can be exempt (i.e., food, medication). People with low incomes can be reimbursed for value-added tax paid through tax credits.

But, as we noted in the previous chapter the United States has no federal sales tax. Alberta's wealth enables that province to do without a sales tax. As a result, Ottawa feels somewhat awkward about the GST. In hopes of winning an election, for instance, the Liberal Party promised to eliminate the GST (once it came to power the promise was shelved). In the same vein, the Conservatives reduced the GST from seven percent to five percent in the hope of turning attention away from the scandal of surpluses generated by the over-taxation of workers through their unemployment insurance contributions—or should I say employment insurance? It was even more surprising to see the Quebec government, after railling for years against fiscal imbalance, refuse to consider using those two percentage points, the least painful tax available, each point of which represented annual revenue of 1.4 billion dollars.[6]

These examples are important for understanding the extent of fiscal leeway allowed in the Canadian federation. In the current situation, however, it is very important to dispel the impression that Quebec taxes people too much, that it borrows too much, and as a result puts its future in jeopardy.

Sources of injustice: taxes on profits

Two aspects of Quebec fiscal policy are problematic and are perceived by the public as a source of injustice. They are: avoidance of taxes on corporate profits and use of tax havens by the rich. Both problems are technical and complicated, yet it is

---

6. Translator's note: Quebec's March 2010 budget included increases in the TVQ.

important to grasp their inner workings to determine whether an independent country, as compared to a province, has the power to control them, at least in theory. Some explanation is necessary; I will attempt to simplify—without being simplistic.

A corporation operating in several countries can, in principle, move its profits wherever taxes are lowest. It can sell goods to a subsidiary at below-market prices, and thereby declare no profits in the country where the goods are produced, but declare profits in the country where they are sold at market prices. Similarly, but in reverse, it can demand exorbitant management fees from its subsidiary, which in turn will declare no profits at all or even declare a loss, while the parent corporation will declare enormous profits. Governments have, of course, developed batteries of regulations to counter roaming profit declarations, but have encountered difficulties in application and enforcement.

In Canada, the provinces have had to deal with the problem of sharing taxes on trans-Canada corporations and banks, as well as insurance, transportation, manufacturing, retail companies and others. The following formula has applied: profits are shared taking the average of each province's shares of sales figures and salaries paid against total sales figures and salaries paid throughout Canada; each province then applies its own tax rate, on profits established using this formula. The problem was supposed to have been solved, that is until the 1976 Quebec elections that brought the Parti Québécois to power. Corporate Canada then began to make its contribution to Canadian unity by transferring profits from Montreal to Toronto. "Sales companies" were set up in Toronto that fictitiously received goods from their Montreal parent companies at low prices (e.g., newsprint) and then sold them at market prices. The same operation was used, but in reverse, to allow profits made at Montreal refineries to be declared in Alberta.

That explains why taxation was modified in 1980. Quebec doubled employer contributions to health services and the tax on capital and in turn substantially reduced tax rates on profits.[7] Corporations could not manipulate the first two tax items, which, in addition, were deductible from taxable income for the federal government. Thus their little games came abruptly to a halt and it became highly advantageous for companies to declare even more profits in Quebec.

The system established in 1980 was so convenient that later governments increased rates across the board, a dangerous step. Caution is in order, especially with capital tax, which can discourage investment.

As an independent country, Quebec would likely be targeted in a similar manner to 1976 after a sovereigntist party won power. It would be even more so after Quebec declared independence. Thought must be given to techniques for countering such actions. These could range from conventional market price auditing techniques to the California formula of determining taxable profits based on the proportion of local sales (in Quebec, for instance), compared to total sales by the company and its subsidiaries.[8]

Tax havens raise completely different problems. Since the world financial crisis and the G20 meeting in November 2008, we have a better grasp of the enormous amounts of money hidden away in tax havens and how the movement of these funds can cause instability. This is a world-scale problem that is now being addressed. But each country must put its house in order before anything can really be accomplished. Canada finds itself in a very uncomfortable position, symbolized by a finance minister, Paul Martin, (who later became Prime Minister), who

---

7. Contribution to health services went from 1.5 percent of total payroll to 3 percent, capital tax, from 0.45 percent to 0.9 percent, while taxes on profits went from 13 percent to 3 percent for small business and 13 percent to 5.5 percent for the others. See *Disours sur le budget*, 1981-1982, pp. 25-26.
8. The California formula was declared illegal, but that would be different for an independent country.

controls Canada's largest shipping company, the Canada Steamship Lines, which is incorporated in Barbados under a fiscal agreement between the two countries that in perfect legality allows his company to pay virtually no taxes.

Sources of injustice: tax havens

Funds are transferred to tax havens in two ways. Some are the outcome of false declarations or illegal transactions, which implies fraud in the country where the funds originated and secrecy in the country that receives them. We have no idea of the amounts involved in fraud, but governments do occasionally reveal the findings of their investigations. In 2009, for example, the United States government called upon the Union Bank of Switzerland to turn over information on the accounts of fifty-two thousand United States citizens suspected of tax fraud.[9]

The other category of transfer stems from existing legislation and tax treaties between countries designed primarily to avoid double taxation. If a Canadian company has already been taxed for its operations in the United States, for example, efforts are made to avoid it being taxed for the same operations in Canada— all of which makes perfect sense.

When Barbados and Canada signed a bilateral tax treaty, Barbadian tax rates were the same as Canada's. It was perfectly normal to recognize that taxes paid in Barbados by Canadian interests should not be taxed again in Canada. It was agreed that payment of taxes owing in Barbados freed the company of tax debt in Canada.

Barbados then proceeded to create special status for international corporations, under which the tax rate was reduced to 2.5 percent. The same principle continued to apply. The Canadian corporation that paid the Barbados rate would pay no tax in

---

9. The United States and Switzerland reached a compromise. Fewer than five thousand accounts were declared.

Canada. In addition, if the funds were placed in a Barbadian trust, no taxes had to be paid at all; the only information required was a local name and an address.

Barbados, with a population of 250,000, quickly became the third most preferred destination for Canadian capital, behind the United States and the United Kingdom. The last time I saw the data, the sums involved exceeded thirty billion dollars. All in perfect legality!

Taxation must be the starting point. For many years, taxation in Quebec, in the areas we are now addressing, has been dependent upon federal taxation in both its design and function. To avoid creating a fiscal jungle, legislation is used to align taxation in Quebec with that of the federal government, with a few exceptions (but sometimes of considerable import).

Once Quebec achieves fiscal autonomy, its taxation will be brought into line with international transactions. After that, Quebec will be able to take part in negotiations now underway. One particularly important issue being addressed is bank secrecy.

Bank secrecy

As a province, Quebec has no influence in drafting the tax treaties signed by Canada. Nor does Quebec participate in ongoing discussions on bank secrecy. Bank secrecy clearly lies at the heart of the issue of legal and illegal capital transfers to tax havens. As I write these lines, it is impossible to fully assess the current situation. A press release issued following April 2009 G20 meeting in London set out a peremptory principle: bank secrecy must end. It expressed a wish, not concrete reality, but it indicated that some movement is underway. We will soon know whether the stated desire for change will prove to be more than just wishful thinking. If real progress is made, it is clear that tax control mechanisms will be revised for those who wish to make serious use of them. They will, in turn, be able to modify their tax treaties accordingly. The exchange of information among countries will make tax control much more effective.

As a province, Quebec has no choice but to go along with whatever Canada decides. As an independent country, Quebec would not be able to go it completely alone. It could not grandstand in Canada's face without sending capital fleeing... However, in practice, Quebec would be able to choose its own models and partners. For example, the United States has much stricter international tax controls than Canada. The underlying issue is the exchange of information and collaboration between real governments of real countries. In the long run, it is simply a question of justice for citizens.

Chapter 12

THE STATE AND THE CITIZEN (PART 2)

This chapter addresses two totally different issues that first appear to have no connection with the economic questions that have played such an important role in my life. Yet they bring me right back to considerations that are closely related to economic development and growth. In short, it is not easy to shake off one's deep personal and collective heritage. These issues are the French language and protection of the environment.

I raise the language question with much reluctance, almost in spite of myself. It is so emotionally loaded and so much at the heart of Quebec's identity that for someone concerned by economic growth and its impact on society, dealing with language is like walking into a minefield, where emotional and even irrational reactions lie in wait. Yet, language, far more than the economy, provokes crises and "moves mountains." It cannot be avoided.

English has become the international language, yet no international legislation brought that about. Quite the opposite in fact; national languages are explicitly protected almost everywhere. The European Union comprises twenty-seven countries and almost twenty-seven languages are used in the European Parliament.[1] Yet English is the common denominator. People do not have to speak it well, but those who master it have

1. Some languages are used by two or more countries. German and French for example.

access to particularly rewarding positions. French played the same role before, like Latin before it. Now it is English.

Live and work in French, but also use English

In all countries, life goes on in the language of the people. In France, for instance, the "Harvard syndrome" has made inroads and people continue to borrow English words massively, such as stubbornly using the word *e-mail* or even *mail* instead of the more logical neologism *courriel,* used in Quebec. Yet daily life in all activities goes on in French, except in sciences where the Harvard syndrome has made serious inroads, and when French multinationals are working in places like China and India. The school system operates in French and people can live and work in France using French only.

The same can be said for all modern, developed countries. People live using their own language, but English offers access to the highest spheres of science, political and business activities. Public education provides a basis in English, but it is up to the individual to carry that knowledge further.

In countries where everybody uses a single language, the above description may seem to be a simplification, but it is not a caricature. The situation is different in countries where several languages coexist. Some countries have reached a workable equilibrium, Switzerland being the prototype. Many reasons explain that country's linguistic stability, and some are not as simple as they might seem. It is nonetheless remarkable that Switzerland has never tried to impose linguistic coexistence and institutional multiculturalism on each canton. Zurich, for instance, has no French-language public schools; Geneva has no German-language public schools; and Lugano, in the Italian section of the country known as Ticino, has neither French nor German-language public schools.

In Belgium, the linguistic battle between Walloons and Flemish continues, with metaphorical shots being fired mainly over the status of Brussels. It is sometimes believed, and even stated, that as societies becomes richer and more modern, tensions ebb and debates of this kind lose their relevance. As Flanders has grown increasingly prosperous—much more so than Wallonia—it has shown astonishing dynamism and no sign of wishing to play down its insistence on defending its language and culture.

The language imbroglio

These issues are complicated at best, and few places are as complicated as Quebec. First of all, two language laws apply. Under the Canadian Constitution, Quebec is officially bilingual. Under Quebec legislation adopted by a federalist government (that of Robert Bourassa), French is Quebec's only official language. The Canadian Constitution imposes upon Quebec an English-language public school system. A college and university education system and a health-care system were also developed, financed on an equal footing with the French-language systems.

As the idea of an independent Quebec took shape, it was inevitable that the goal of making French the true language of Quebec would come to the fore. People wanted a country and they wanted that country to have a language. Bill 101 was closely linked to Quebec sovereignty. It asserted the predominance of French, yet maintained English as an acquired right for individuals. People who themselves had attended English schools in Quebec had the right to send their children to English schools. Public signage had to ensure the predominance of French. Businesses had to adopt the French language and obtain a certificate attesting to their Francization.

The 1980 referendum defeat followed shortly after the French Language Charter (Bill 101) was adopted, but René Lévesque's government was reelected a year later. Debate raged for several years before the courts, which gradually reduced the scope of

Bill 101 at a time when the Quebec government was struggling to stay afloat.

The Quebec clause on schooling was replaced by the Canada clause, which meant that children whose parents had attended an English school in Canada could attend English schools. To protect the use of English on commercial signs, a new right was created: henceforth, the Charter of Rights protected the freedom of conscience and speech for companies as well as for individuals. In addition, it came as no surprise that companies operating under federal jurisdiction were exempted from the obligation to comply with the French Language Charter. They included banks, transportation companies of all kinds (airlines, marine, pipelines, highway transport—if trucks crossed provincial or international borders), radio and television broadcasting, and Crown corporations and agencies.

The achievements of Bill 101

Despite the legal obstacles and the two referendum defeats, the French Language Charter did achieve some major objectives. Since its adoption, most immigrant children go to French primary and secondary schools. French is the language of commercial signs, even though use of English on the signs does not always comply with the law. In practical terms, French is now the language used in everyday life, except for certain neighbourhoods in Montreal's west end. Young people in Quebec might not be aware of the progress, but for people of my generation the contrast between before and after Bill 101 is staggering.

The language of work remains a problem. Discussion of this question requires more than a little caution, given the complexity of the question. Although I have been involved for years with companies either as a consultant or as a board member, my view is necessarily limited.

No longer do we see companies negotiating collective agreements in English with English-speaking business agents that result in an English document for workers a majority of whom do not even speak English. No, I have not invented this story. One of the triggers that led to Bill 101 was pulled when René Lévesque received a report from a leader of the Steelworkers who described the situation exactly as I have. With the adoption of language legislation by normal democratic means, multi-nationals adapted, as they do everywhere else. Obviously, there are exceptions: Wal-Mart is not known to lose any sleep when it violates the labour code. Overall, however, ensuring that foreign companies comply with local legislation is not the most serious challenge.

The massive entry of French-speaking people into the business world, not because of Bill 101 but after its adoption, completely changed the picture. Some of the stars of the new generation of entrepreneurs felt that they were taking revenge on history: they took pride at having conquered a place for themselves, in economic terms, in the Americas, and in the world, without turning their backs on their roots and culture. The context is not always favourable. A biological research company whose financial structure includes an American venture capital fund, for example, may have to conduct clinical trials to be submitted to the United States Food and Drug Administration. If those trials are conducted in some twenty North American hospitals of which only two are French-speaking institutions, obtaining a Francization certificate can be a daunting challenge. I once sat on the board of directors of such a firm with only one unilingual English-speaking member, but who was also chairman of the board. Everything had to be translated into French, minutes, technical notes, and so forth. All the meetings were conducted in English. Obviously, one day, somebody ended up proposing that for economic reasons it would be better to produce only English documentation. With the confidence that comes from the public office that I once held, I stated, without being sure I was on solid ground, that it would be illegal. The issue never came up again.

Being part of North America

The more Quebec businesses develop their international relations, particularly in North America, the more complicated it will be to establish the proper regulatory and legislative balance with respect to French. The problem is compounded by a double system of laws whose application depends on whether the business falls in federal or Quebec jurisdiction. Another example will help illustrate this point. Lévesque-Beaubien has developed into the largest French-language brokerage firm. When I was appointed finance minister, I appointed it to head the syndicate mandated to issue Quebec government and Hydro-Québec bonds in Canadian dollars, which in fact only consolidated the role that the firm had played for generations in Quebec society.

The National Bank, another large French-language institution under federal jurisdiction, thus legally bound to official bilingualism, acquired Lévesque-Beaubien, which then bought First Marathon, a Toronto brokerage firm bound to comply with Ontario legislation that allowed it to operate in English only. Since then, thousands of Quebec customers of the merged company, now known as National Bank Financial, receive most of their securities analyses in English only.

Anecdotes like these are not intended to belittle legislative tools to regulate the language of business, nor to downplay the certification role of Quebec's language monitoring agency, the Office de la langue française. My only purpose is to demonstrate the limits of legislation. For many business people, especially among those who speak English, "the language question was settled in 1995!" Others have understood that if a company employs fewer than fifty people, it can do as it pleases. For still others, there is no point in "being more Catholic than the pope." Since the current government is not worked up about the French language, Bill 101 is perceived as a partisan political issue.

This confusion obviously has repercussions on the integration of immigrants into Quebec society, which takes place primarily in the workplace. Legislation has successfully brought children of immigrants into the French school system and as a result French is becoming their day-to-day language, but confusion abounds in the workplace and English still exerts tremendous pressure.

When Quebec is an independent country, much of the language imbroglio will untangle itself naturally. But that remains abstract. It must become clear to everyone that French is a language of power and money. Quebec-controlled multinationals, financial institutions and government-owned corporations will have a key role to play. From the standpoint of the French language, the question of whether control of large corporations remains in Montreal or moves to Toronto or New York is far from a trivial one. The fact that research in new technologies in Quebec remains high and that the government apparatus, universities and large decision-making centres operate in French are vital factors. This is the only way to persuade workers, citizens, immigrants, and everybody else that French is Quebec's real language and not only the language spoken by those who have no ambition and who do not succeed in life.

Until the national question is settled

Until the national question is settled and Quebec can attain a somewhat normal political status, the advancement of French will essentially depend on the will of the people who hold power in the Quebec government. The success with which immigrants are integrated will be determined by the emphasis placed on language questions and the quality of the organization responsible for it. Applying Bill 101 to businesses with less than fifty employees might simply be wishful thinking, or it could lead to a realistic implementation plan that is different from the one applied to large companies that has proven effective. Preventing the children of immigrants from attending English Cegeps when they are already young adults appears complicated to me. The idea of eliminating English Cegeps is unrealistic, but there must be a way to better prepare students attending them to live and work in French in Quebec.

The importance of amending Quebec's language legislation should not be played down. Yet my belief is that the needed changes cannot be brought about while Quebec is still a province. They can only take place when there is a clear will to make French not only the common language but also the language that is necessary in order to succeed in Quebec.

Climate change: the top priority

As the market emerges from the financial and economic crisis that began at the end of 2007, the dominant issue before the crisis, namely climate change, will come to the fore once more. Global warming is now recognized as a fact, just as human activity is recognized as a cause. President Obama's election put an end to the global-warming denial of his predecessor. The speed with which the Arctic sea-ice sheet is melting, much more rapidly than scientific projections, is frightening. If such egregious errors are possible, what are our projections on the impact of climate change on agriculture and water resources worth?

The world's leading powers rapidly reached an agreement on the financial crisis. The world banking system had to be rescued. At first, there was some hesitation as to whether the central banks or the finance ministries should purchase the "toxic" financial products or become equity shareholders. Agreement was reached rapidly on recovery programs, and collective efforts were made to avoid returning to protectionism (though some excesses were tolerated).[2]

Climate change is another story. Although it is impossible to examine the issue fully here, a look at some of the opposing and

---

2. For instance, the Buy American clause applicable to states and cities in the United States.

diverging interests will help us grasp the framework in which a small country like Quebec will have to establish its policies.

The Montreal Protocol was the first multilateral agreement on control of greenhouse gas emissions into the atmosphere. It was adopted in 1987 to protect the ozone layer by prohibiting the use of chlorofluorocarbons and other substances that attack that layer. Practically speaking, it meant prohibiting aerosol sprays then, and it turned out to be remarkably successful. A joint World Trade Organization-United Nations Environment Program publication reported: "It is estimated that the [Montreal] Protocol will have decreased the contribution of ODS [ozone-depleting substances] emissions to climate change by 135 GtCO2-eq over the 1990 to 2010 period. This means that the Montreal Protocol has achieved four to five times greater levels of climate mitigation than the target contemplated by the first commitment period under the Kyoto Protocol."[3]

Kyoto

That early realization of what a multinational agreement could accomplish created illusions. Spectacular results, it was thought, could be achieved at little cost. When the question of global warming was addressed directly, however, the contradiction between control of greenhouse gas emissions and economic growth became clear. Atmospheric temperatures had increased because of emissions from fossil fuels, oil, coal and natural gas, in short, carbon emissions. To prevent temperatures from reaching levels that could transform the world as we know it, greenhouse gases (expressed in CO2 equivalent) must be reduced. Stabilizing them is not enough; radical reductions must be considered. The Kyoto Protocol was the first clear international manifestation of a will to reduce greenhouse gas emissions. It was signed in 1997 but it took several years to obtain ratification

---

3. WTO and UNEP, *Trade and Climate Change*, Geneva, WTO, 2009, p. XV.

by fifty-five countries required to enforce the protocol. The process had begun in 1990, when the International Panel on Climate Change (IPCC) was created, which in turn led to the 1992 United Nations Framework Convention on Climate Change reached at the Earth Summit in Rio de Janeiro.

It took five more years to reach the Kyoto accord with a greenhouse gas emission reduction objective of 5.2 percent below 1990 levels. It was clear that diverging interests were at play. Emerging countries led by China and India demanded, and obtained, exoneration from any obligations based on the principle that could be summed up as follows: "You rich countries have polluted the atmosphere for two centuries. It is up to you to clean up the mess you have made. Let us develop economically as you have." Their argument was accepted at Kyoto.

Europe, which has limited oil and natural gas reserves (except in the North Sea) and which has shut down most of its coalmines, enthusiastically embraced Kyoto's constraining objectives. The six-percent reduction goal was flexibly divided up among European Union members. Increases were allowed for some countries, others were allowed to maintain 1990 levels, while the majority of countries had to reduce emissions.

The United States did not ratify the treaty. For President George W. Bush, environmental protection was clearly an obstacle to economic growth. It was also clear that China, in addition to all of its other competitive advantages, should not enjoy an exemption from meeting any greenhouse gas emission reduction goals at a time when the United States was expected to meet the Kyoto Protocol constraints.

Canada had already ratified Kyoto when the Conservatives took power in 2006. If Kyoto were to apply, the development and exploitation of Alberta tar sands would have to slow down or become much more costly. That was too much to ask of the Conservatives whose base is in the West; they were not about to make such a sacrifice. The Canadian government therefore attempted to square the circle by not implementing Kyoto but claiming that an alternative formula would produce the same or similar results. Nobody was fooled.

Politicians tail public opinion

On climate change, the public is ahead of politicians almost everywhere; people are convinced that temperatures are rising and that the consequences may well be devastating. Above all, throughout the world, citizens believe that they can help and that they have a role to play in "saving the planet." For more than fifty years I have been involved in public activities, as a teacher, an economist or a politician, and I do not remember having ever seen young people get so interested and involved in an issue. Most of all, I never thought I would see so many people demonstrate their commitment so keenly by taking personal initiatives that, if taken alone, would be trivial but which, taken as a whole, show a collective desire for a better world. In Quebec, this collective desire has been demonstrated in many ways for many years. Since the early 1980s, people living near lakes have monitored water quality, imposed shoreline protection measures and septic field controls, and curbed blue-green algae development, all in an aim to ensure that *their* water remains potable. In schools, teachers initiate children to the leading environmental issues as well as to all the small actions that can be taken to support the common good. Their parents sometimes take to the streets to demonstrate their opposition to specific projects that, in their opinion, threaten the environment and their quality of life, which is the real reward for their political activism. This type of action has taken place in different shapes and forms throughout the world, peacefully, for the most part, except for occasional clashes when some people get the impression that governments are blinded or manipulated by oil, coal or financial interests working behind the scenes.

Quebec gets involved

In Europe where this kind of behind-the-scenes pressure is less effective, the voice of environmental concern is more easily heard. In North America, where the states and provinces belong to larger federations, there has been a move to use the inherent flexibility, first in the United States, and then on both sides of the border, to link state and provincial governments in greenhouse gas reduction programs, which public opinion perceives to be the heart of the fight for maintaining the quality of the environment. California became a type of laboratory, with the New England states also showing leadership. Quebec has not been far behind, and in some ways became the centre of debate. Here is a short background summary published in Quebec's 2006-2012 action plan entitled *Quebec and Climate Change* published in June 2006. "The emissions reduction target that Quebec wants to achieve is the one it already committed to in 2001 under the Climate Change Action Plan of the Conference of New England Governors and Eastern Canadian Premiers. Quebec then undertook to contribute to achieving the regional greenhouse gas reduction target, that is ten percent below the 1990 levels by 2020. This Action Plan 2006-2012 is the first step taken to achieve that goal."[4]

The Action Plan 2006-2012 published in June 2006 referred directly to Kyoto. A carbon tax in the form of a pollution surcharge on the sale of oil and gas products was imposed and is expected to bring in two hundred million dollars annually. Twenty-three measures were instituted to reduce emissions to 1.5 percent below 1990 levels. Pressure on the federal government exerted by a unanimous Quebec National Assembly and by many civil society representatives resulted in a federal transfer to Quebec of three hundred and fifty million dollars. This led in

---

4. Translated from the French action plan published in 2006. To consult Quebec's action plan, see *Quebec and Climate Change. A Challenge for the Future,* Action Plan 2006-2012, June 2008.

turn to a new action plan in 2008, an increase in the number of measures, and greenhouse gas emissions reductions to six percent below 1990 levels, thus meeting the Kyoto target.

It is not certain whether or not that target will be met. It is remarkable, nonetheless, that each year a progress report is published and people can closely monitor the progress of a truly Quebec program that has little to do with a vague and yet-to-be-defined Canadian program. But how to find a common denominator between Alberta's annual per capita greenhouse gas emissions of seventy-one tons (CO_2 equivalent) and Quebec's eleven tons of annual per capita emissions?[5]

A carbon exchange was scheduled to be a part of the Montreal stock exchange, as consolation after its sale to the Toronto Stock Exchange, but it is inactive except for the odd speculative transaction. The Canadian government is opposed to production quotas and constraining commitments, and its position did not change at the Copenhagen Conference in December 2009. While President Bush was in office, Canada's position on climate change seemed comfortable. The American position has changed under President Obama who agrees in principle that the post-Kyoto period must include constraints. To bring American public opinion to support that position, China and India must also be brought into the agreement—but that is likely to prove a delicate and challenging operation. The compromise reached at the May 2009 meeting in Washington showed that not too much could be expected. China and India would be part of the post-Kyoto agreement which would be based on two notions: global warming should not exceed two degrees and greenhouse gas emissions reductions would apply to 2050, i.e., after most of the signatories had died. The secretary general of the United Nations was very disappointed.[6]

---

5. The Canadian per capita average is 23 tons. See Chapter 9, p. 170.
6. Translator's note: The book was published on November 16, 2009, before the Copenhagen Conference.

Despite the vagueness of international negotiations, it is striking to see how Quebec is in a position either to join, on a voluntary basis, the efforts of leading countries in the struggle to limit greenhouse gas emissions or to apply quickly a system of constraints if the international community so decides. The law adopted unanimously by the National Assembly on June 18, 2008, is outstanding in this regard. These are the explanatory notes accompanying the bill entitled: *An Act to amend the Environment Quality Act and other legislative provisions in relation to climate change.*

> The purpose of this Act is to reduce greenhouse gas emissions, which affect the quality of the atmosphere and contribute to global warming and climate change.
>
> Under this Act, the Minister may require that emitters determined by regulation of the Minister report their greenhouse gas emissions for the purposes of a greenhouse gas emissions inventory. The information reported by emitters is to be kept in a public register.
>
> This Act prescribes that the Minister prepare a climate change action plan and submit it to the Government. It also requires the yearly publication by the Minister of a greenhouse gas emissions inventory and of a report on the measures implemented to reduce greenhouse gas emissions and to fight climate change.
>
> This Act provides that the Government is to set greenhouse gas reduction targets using 1990 emissions as the baseline.
>
> It also contains various provisions allowing the Government to put in place, by regulation, all the mechanisms required to implement a cap-and-trade system.
>
> In addition, it requires that certain emitters cover their greenhouse gas emissions with an equivalent number of emission allowances, whether emission units, offset credits or early reduction credits, which may be traded and banked under the cap-and-trade system. Caps on the number of emission units the Minister may grant are to be set by the Government.
>
> This Act contains various other provisions relating to the management and operation of the cap-and-trade system—including delegation of its management to a third party—and to its harmon-

ization and integration with similar systems implemented by other authorities.

Lastly, this Act provides that sums collected under the new provisions are to be used to finance various climate change measures.[7]

This legislation adopted by the province of Quebec could easily be that of an independent country. Though it would undoubtedly be applied differently, its principles and goals are those of a country.

Environment prevails over the WTO

Quebec's political status becomes an important issue once it is recognized that international environmental agreements prevail over trade agreements. The document published jointly by the World Trade Organization and the United Nations Environment Program clearly establishes that "WTO case law has confirmed that WTO rules do not override environmental requirements."[8]

This means that international environmental agreements prevail over World Trade Organization agreements. If Canada persists in refusing to abide by rules to limit greenhouse gases, the international community or certain member countries could take retaliatory measures, claiming that by its refusal to apply internationally agreed upon rules the Canadian government is providing domestic producers with a discriminatory competitive advantage. Penalties could even be imposed on Canada. If this threat were to materialize, Canada would have to choose between, on the one hand, maintaining current oil and gas exploitation conditions and agreeing to pay the cost of retaliatory measures or internationally imposed penalties, or, on the other hand, reducing greenhouse gas emissions enough to avoid paying those penalties.[9] The choice would be based on economic calculations.

---

7. National Assembly, *An Act to amend the Environment Quality Act and other legislative provisions in relation to climate change*, Quebec, Government of Quebec, 2009, p. 2.
8. WTO and UNEP, Trade and Climate Change, *op. cit.*, p. XIX.
9. Another way to control greenhouse gas levels would be to purchase pollution rights on the international market.

Quebec as a province would have no choice at all. It has no way of defending itself against the costs it would have to bear, and would have no calculations to make.

It is to be hoped, of course, that Canada will finally agree to international rules, but if it refuses to do so in order to profit from very high oil prices, Quebec would have no way of protecting itself... unless of course it pulled out of Canada and took advantage of its excellent situation and the measures already in place. This presents an interesting case. Whether Quebec is a province or an independent country, its greenhouse gas reduction program is the same, or more precisely, can be the same. However, if Canada continues to drag its feet with respect to the international community, Quebec has every reason to become an independent country.

CONCLUSION

As we conclude our overview, one conclusion that lies at the heart of the debate on Quebec independence stands out. After all the years of debate and study and the political ebbs and flows, a majority of Quebecers still believe that Quebec sovereignty is desirable and viable, but a majority of Quebecers also think it will not happen. In both cases, the majority is substantial. How can the optimism, self-assurance, and confidence in the future be restored? The question is a tough one. Too many people are pessimistic, convinced that the difficulties are insurmountable, that projects undertaken are never carried through to completion. Many young people have come to believe that they will not enjoy their parents' standard of living. Some of Quebec's greatest success stories are in crisis: education reform—the foremost achievement of the Quiet Revolution—has resulted in shocking dropout levels; the Caisse de dépôt et placement, custodian of a large portion of Quebecers' savings, suffered enormous losses in 2008, which clashes with the image of prudence and cautious management that should be the hallmark of such an institution.

A technician's viewpoint

The future often appears to us to be gloomy, difficult, beset by obstacles. Quebec's aging population and it indebtedness are perceived as insurmountable barriers, not just for an independent Quebec but for Quebec under whatever status.

Yet Quebec has been less affected by the current recession than Ontario, Western Canada, and most regions in the United States. Quebec has also fared very well in comparison with other countries in the world. Although very real problems demand solutions, none defies our ability to solve them as long as a little willpower and the appropriate mechanisms are brought to bear.

That is the technician's viewpoint, but the technician has little influence in a society that is tired of being thrown from pillar to post by two conflicting political options.

We are torn between two countries and two governments. One is intent on keeping Quebec in Canada and is prepared to use all the means it sees fit to do so. The other government adopts positions that are inspired by a sense of belonging, either to Canada or to Quebec. When federalists are in office in Quebec City, they attempt to keep their distance from the federal government in order to avoid appearing to be a simple agency of it. When sovereigntists hold power, they work to achieve sovereignty while seeking to show that pursuit of their goal does not prevent them from governing Quebec well.

The identity problem

This situation amplifies the difficulties Quebecers experience in defining who they are. The identity problem changes from one generation to another but remains crucial. People in my father's generation were born as *Canadiens*, as opposed to the *Anglais*. In the middle of the twentieth century, they were French Canadians, as opposed to the English Canadians. Many of them came to see themselves at the end of their lives as Quebecers, as opposed to Canadians. Their national anthem "Ô Canada," which they sang proudly to distinguish themselves from those who sang "God save the King"—or Queen—became a national anthem for Canadians, and left them without one.

Three identities in the course of a single lifetime! Today's generations face different identity problems. Given the choice of being Canadians, French Canadians or Quebecers, a majority of them choose to be Quebecers. Yet in their ever more numerous contacts with other countries, they must also be Canadians. At every turn in their lives, from teaching through research, volunteer activity, municipal funding, publishing support, arts and sports, to the installation of Internet links in rural areas, they are exposed to the largesse of the federal government that doles out money in a unceasing effort to outdo the Quebec government.

These factors combine to make the identity question into a trap. It has become suspicious for Quebecers to use the term "nous" (we). Does this "nous" exclude those who speak English, or immigrants, or Muslims? Perhaps it is proof that old-stock Quebecers are racist? The Bouchard-Taylor Commission, whose hearings were broadcast by CBC on prime time, had all the trappings of a provocation, and might have caused serious problems in a less peaceful country.

A few clear ideas

The identity issue must be taken by the horns guided by a few clear ideas that must never be imposed. Allow me to suggest a few of my own. Quebecers, to the best of my knowledge, readily accept the notion that "a Quebecer is someone who wants to be a Quebecer." Those who do not want to be Quebecers still enjoy the full protection of the Charter of Rights. Questions of religious or cultural specificity (e.g., the burka, kirpan in schools, etc.) will have to be settled as in all other countries, but collective self-flagellation is not required.

The old-stock English-speaking population enjoys acquired rights that do not include the right to anglicize new immigrants.

French is the official language and the language generally used.

Immigrants must have access to well-organized support facilities for learning French and also to ensure they are introduced to Quebec culture and history. For young people, integration takes place in the schools. But immigrants of whatever age should receive efficient and effective services. It was a mistake, for instance, to abandon the Centres d'orientation et de formation des immigrants (COFI).

The teaching of history is vital and lies at the heart of political debate. Shortly after the October crisis in 1970, the Liberal government dropped compulsory history courses at school under the pretext they helped train "separatists." Only when the Parti Québécois was elected in 1976 was history restored in schools, but then only partially. When I was elected premier in 1994, the importance of history in school curriculums was reassessed. In recent years, a new history course appeared under the Liberal government. In the initial version, the central theme consisted in presenting the relationship between the English and the French in Canada, and in Quebec, as a Sunday afternoon drive in the country. Anything that alluded to conflict was eliminated. Rapid and widespread indignation forced the government to back down.

This type of foolishness has to end. The school is the crucible of the nation. It is there that shared values are transmitted, alongside knowledge.

Integration would obviously be easier in a country that has clearly defined itself. But this has become a vicious circle, in which our inability to settle the identity question prevents us from settling the national question; and since we have not succeeded in deciding on our political status, we continue fighting over how we are to define ourselves. That vicious circle needs to be broken; we need to agree on what political orientation should be given to our collective-spirited, democratic French-speaking society in North America that has created a culture as original as it is universal.

Translating values into projects

To desire to build a country means that values must be translated into projects. Equality of opportunity must be defined through the transformation of our school system. Full employment in today's world implies, as has been shown, major changes in manpower training and adaptation to changes in the workplace. Creating wealth necessarily requires an aptitude to compete on international markets. That is a condition for increasing income and wellbeing. Creating wealth is one step, but it must be accompanied by the equitable distribution of wealth. The former involves a host of technical considerations, while the latter assumes a variety of forms depending on what is perceived as socially just. The aging population will have many repercussions that we are only beginning to examine. The fact that a large number of people will live more than twenty years in good health after what has long been considered as the usual retirement age will have more impacts than simply increasing health costs, which appears to be the main subject of interest with regard to retirement costs.

The list goes on depending on people's interests. A society that grows wealthier must be able to humanize and personalize social services for those affected by illness or physical or mental handicaps. The same society must also provide an intense cultural life.

It is imperative to set goals that take all of society's resources into full account. We have never had the opportunity to do that in Quebec, whether it be for our children or for the elderly, for economic development or culture. We have never been able to establish an overarching vision, and the one-upmanship of our two governments has been far from helpful on that score. In an increasing number of activities or programs, we end up not really knowing who does what.

If in one area of activity the programs established by both governments are complementary and support one another, then all is well. If not, the devil takes the hindmost. Overlapping has reached the point that, whatever the issue, citizens have a hard time knowing where to turn and knowing who is responsible for what.

People need to know

That is why the sovereignty movement must absolutely develop programs for governing an independent Quebec even before it wins the election. The 1995 experience has taught us many rich lessons. Studies were initiated before the 1994 election and the newly created restructuration ministry set to work immediately, but time was lacking. The avalanche of studies and reports issued during the months leading up to the referendum campaign created an image of disorder that did far more harm than good.

People must know where their political leaders intend to lead them and what they intend to do. I will never forget one radio hotline conversation before the referendum. A woman asked:

"Is the Criminal Code federal responsibility?"

"Yes, Ma'am," I answered.

"Well when we are independent, what will we do with thieves?" she asked.

"The National Assembly will adopt a law making the Criminal Code a Quebec law. Then, when we want to change it, such as for young offenders, the National Assembly will adopt the necessary amendments."

"Now I understand," she said, "thank you very much."

For questions that affect them, citizens must be able to see how the question is presented, what the international constraints are, what the government is proposing to do, and what the oppositions thinks, before they make up their minds. Moaning, groaning, and complaining will come to an end, as will the habit of blaming the federal government for everything that goes wrong. Quebecers will have their own country.

The last sentence in my introduction reads as follows: "The conclusion returns to what I have always considered as the most profound and essential reason for Quebec to become an independent country: for the Quebec people to assume full responsibility for themselves in a democracy in which the state is fully answerable to its citizens."

So here I am, back where I began.

STATEMENTS BY JACQUES CHIRAC, PRESIDENT OF FRANCE, AND BILL CLINTON, PRESIDENT OF THE UNITED STATES, BEFORE THE 1995 REFERENDUM

Jacques Chirac on Larry King Live, CNN, Monday, October 23 1995.

To a viewer who called from Montreal to ask a question, Jacques Chirac replied: "The French government does not want to interfere with this referendum." Larry King then asked: "But if Quebec does vote to separate, will you recognize them?" Jacques Chirac replied: "We'll see... We yes, of course, we would recognize the fact."

Statement made by President Clinton at the White House on Tuesday, October 24 1995, in reply to a question asked by a Canadian journalist from the *Globe and Mail:*

"Let me give you a careful answer. When I was in Canada last year, I said that I thought that Canada had served as a model to the United States and to the entire world about how people of different cultures could live together in harmony, respecting their differences but working together. This vote is a Canadian internal issue for the Canadian people to decide. And I would not presume to interfere with that. I can tell you that a strong and united Canada has been a wonderful partner for the United States and incredibly important and constructive citizen throughout the entire world. Just since I've been president, I have seen how our partnership works, how the leadership of Canada in so many ways throughout the world works, and what it means to the rest of the world to think that there's a country like Canada where things basically work. Everybody's got problems, but it looks like a country that's doing the right things, moving in the right direction, has the kinds of values that we'd all be proud of. And they have been a strong and powerful ally of ours. And I have to tell you that I hope we'll be able to continue that. I have to say that I hope that will continue. That's been good for the United States. Now the people of Quebec will have to cast their votes as their lights guide them. But Canada has been a great model for the rest of the world and has been a partner for the United States, and I hope that can continue."

DISINFORMATION

Propaganda plays a major role in maintaining a climate of anxiety. It is the inevitable outcome when the media are controlled by a small number of people and by the federal government. When most "decision-makers" have the same point of view on a fundamental political issue, propaganda takes over. There's not much that can be done. It's like a hailstorm. You just wait until it calms down.

Examples of disinformation abound. One recent case concerned Slovakia's separation from the Czech Republic in 1992, which caused headaches for Canadian federalists.

A country became independent following a simple vote in Parliament, and with the agreement of the Czechs who were nonetheless upset. Assets and debt were divided quickly. There was no violence. "We're finally in our own home," said the Slovaks. "Good riddance," said the Czechs.

A few months before our referendum in 1995, Slovakia suddenly became a hot issue for the big names in the Canadian and Quebec media. The *Globe and Mail* published several strongly worded editorial warnings on the subject. Radio-Canada sent one of its leading reporters to investigate for the flagship program *Le Point*. For a while, pundits in our media were strikingly unanimous in their opinions on Slovakia. As if in one voice they observed that the Slovak economy was smaller than the Czech economy and thus more fragile, unemployment was higher in Slovakia, the monetary union so dear to Slovaks had collapsed, the Czechs would close their market to the Slovaks, and so on. The message was clear: "Quebecers must be careful not to fall into that terrible trap."

Slovakia then, as if by magic, disappeared completely from the media. It was no longer of any use to the federalist cause. A few months later, I received a long analysis prepared by the Morgan Guaranty Trust Research Department published in London and entitled: *Slovakia: Is Rapid Growth Sustainable?* One subtitle read: "Slovak Economy Continues to Impress."

I can understand why they were impressed. In 1995, Slovakia's economy, in real terms, grew at a rate of seven percent, one of the highest rates among all European countries. In 1994, the growth rate had been six percent. Exports were strong as was domestic consumer activity and Slovakia sold more goods to the Czech Republic than it purchased.

In short, everything we were being told was false! But the truth was of no importance after all. What counted then was to ensure that the No side won the 1995 referendum.

INDEX OF PROPER NAMES

Recycled
Supporting responsible use
of forest resources
www.fsc.org Cert no. SGS-COC-003153
© 1996 Forest Stewardship Council

FSC

MARQUIS

Marquis Book Printing Inc.

Québec, Canada
2010

Printed on Silva Enviro which contains 100% recycled post-consumer fibre,
is EcoLogo, Processed Chlorine Free and manufactured using biogas energy.